How to Win
(& Survive)
a Lawsuit

~The Secrets Revealed~

How to Win (& Survive) a Lawsuit

~The Secrets Revealed~

Robert M. Dawson

arbor books

For further information, please contact the author at:
rmdawson@fulbright.com

Book design by,
Arbor Books, Inc.
19 Spear Road, Suite 202
Ramsey, NJ 07446
www.arborbooks.com

Printed in the United States

How to Win & Survive a Lawsuit
Robert M. Dawson
 1. Title 2. Author 3. Law / Practical Guide

Library of Congress Control Number: 2006930965
ISBN: 0-9786107-4-1

Acknowledgements

All that I know as a lawyer must be largely attributed
to the extraordinary colleagues and partners that I
have been honored to collaborate with throughout
my career, and I am indebted to the
wisdom and mentoring of many.

~

All that I am I owe to my entire family,
whose support and values sustain me in
every aspect of my life.

~

I would like to dedicate this book to my daughters,
Michelle and Stephanie, who inspire me
everyday to reach a little higher.

~

Finally, I gratefully acknowledge the important
contributions of Kathy Brandenburg to this work.

.

Table of Contents

Why You May Be Reading This

A lawsuit is a war, and wise people go to war only as a last resort. If you are ever involved in a lawsuit, the odds are that you will be angry, or scared, or both. Being in a lawsuit is usually a difficult experience, and sometimes it is a nightmare. If you find yourself in a lawsuit, either because you have to sue someone or because someone sues you, this book will help you come out in one piece, and will also help you "win." Whatever side of the lawsuit you are on, you want it to end the best way possible in terms of your health, your piece of mind, and your financial condition. You want to "win," and you want to know what winning will mean. Life is short, and you don't want this lawsuit to suck all of the oxygen out of it. You want to have as much control as possible of your case as it travels through a legal system that is often confusing, even infuriating. All of this is true whether you are an individual, a small business, or a big company. Here is the good news: Understanding the simple principles explained in this book will help. The secrets revealed here are real, and they are really important.

This book begins by answering most of the basic questions that people have about lawsuits. Then, it explains the three key phases of a lawsuit, how to evaluate your case, how to plan and strategize your case, and how to win your case by getting a good settlement or by winning a trial.

I.

Your First Questions

Chapter 1

Why Are Lawyers Such Jerks

Actually, most of them are not, but many people have the impression that lawyers are typically unpleasant. Like all aspects of the legal system, our impressions of lawyers are often shaped by television and film. However, beyond Hollywood, we also hear many unflattering "real life" lawyer stories. Why? Here is the secret to lawyers: They just want clients. If you are a client, they are usually happy to be whoever you want them to be. And who do you want them to be? Now that, interestingly, is where the search for the answer to the question posed by this chapter begins.

Most people will tell you that, in general, they want lawyers to be honest, sincere, and fair-minded. That is, most people who aren't in a lawsuit will tell you that. As soon as these same kind people are suing their employer, or getting divorced, or being sued after an accident, they are looking for the meanest, toughest, most ruthless "great" lawyer in town, the sort that only eats raw meat and laughs at the pain of others, to "go get" their opponent. If all people wanted to be represented by Gregory Peck in *To Kill a Mockingbird*, then more lawyers would try to fit that image. I once was asked, in an initial interview by a prospective client, "Are you a lover, or are you a fighter?" I was too politic to tell him what a stupid question this was. To my credit or shame, he did hire me. We usually are who you want us to be.

It is true that some lawyers are an embarrassment to the profession, and to our society. Many others are good and decent people who try, with all the professionalism they can muster, to help the people who are counting on them. A few, like the late Leon Jaworski, transform our society and our system of justice through their ability and character. Mr. Jaworski is best remembered for his role as the Special Prosecutor in the Watergate Scandal, selected by the White House after it had fired former Special Prosecutor Archibald Cox. He then did his job and caused President Nixon's resignation. He is also remembered as a Chief Prosecutor at the War Crimes trials in Europe following the Second World War. Perhaps his greatest achievement, however, was in 1962, when, as the leader of what was then a southern law firm, he accepted the task of prosecuting the Governor of Mississippi for blocking the efforts of James Meredith to attend the University of Mississippi. It may be difficult to appreciate today the courage that it took, in that time and place, to accept this assignment. Jaworski received numerous threats, and required 24-hour police protection. His law firm lost clients, and he and his partners were shunned and despised by some in their community; his partners stood with him, and he never relented in his task nor regretted accepting it. We lawyers do have some good role models. Character matters.

Lawyers are important because they are critical actors in a legal system that separates our society from societies that are dominated by terror and chaos. Any society that is backward, repressive, or uncivilized is a society that, first and foremost, desperately needs an organized body of law and a system of justice. At their best, lawyers make society better. At their worst, they exacerbate arguments and complicate our lives needlessly. One thing is certain— they never operate in a vacuum. They work for us. The criticism of lawyers is a bit like the criticism of Congress. Most people hate Congress, but they tend to like their own Congressperson. Their Congressperson gets expensive benefits for their district, while Congress as a whole wastes money. Many people never see the connection. In a free society, the buck always stops with all of us.

One important point needs to be emphasized, a point which hopefully will be made clear by much of what follows in this book. Just because your lawyer is acting "aggressively" does not mean that he is doing a good job. Just because a lawyer is behaving in a classy or cordial manner, does not mean that he is weak, or that he is not fighting fiercely for every advantage on your behalf. There are many different "styles" that can be equally effective, and there are great lawyers who are always intense and aggressive, while other equally great lawyers appear more calm and reserved. What every good lawyer understands is that being "aggressive"—which is absolutely necessary to fight for you as we must and want to do—is more subtle than just appearing aggressive. Some lawyers who seem to come right out of central casting, and who work too hard at presenting an intimidating image, are in fact lousy lawyers who are getting lousy results for their clients. There is no question that your lawyer's job is to be intensely aggressive about getting you the result that you want. In my experience, however, most truly great lawyers can play more than one note. They are equally comfortable being gracious and diplomatic, or intensely combative when that is required.

Chapter 2

How The Legal System Works; And Doesn't Work

A Trial Is A Story

You figure out pretty quickly when you go to trial that what actually happened doesn't matter. All that matters is what the jury is told about what happened. And there is often a significant difference between those two. When you are in a trial, you are telling your story. Your story is often only as good as your weakest storyteller, just like a chain is as strong as its weakest link. As your case begins, you and your lawyer must focus, first, on what story you will try to tell, and how you will tell it. You must start seeing the facts of your dispute through the eyes of the judge and the jury, who will only hear (and evaluate) the witnesses who are presented to them, and the documents that they are shown. It is based upon this, the evidence, that they will try to figure out what happened, and who is right. They are the audience of a theatrical re-creation, directed by your lawyer, of the drama that led to the lawsuit. If the jury doesn't trust your key storyteller, or doesn't like you, or doesn't hear or see a critical part of the drama because you can't obtain admissible evidence on that point, then what "actually" happened won't matter nearly as much as you would like it to.

You can't change the facts, and you can't control completely what the jury will hear. However, because a trial is a story, there are factors basic to the art of story-telling which <u>are</u> in your control, and which can have a significant impact on what the jury understands and believes. What these factors are, and how they can be controlled, is what we want to focus on here. It all comes down to what every good storyteller understands: you can't confuse your audience, and you can't bore your audience. Like a good book, your story must have a clear plot, it must be interesting, and it must be understandable. You must tie the beginning, middle, and end of the story together, so that the audience follows the story, and knows where you are in the story. All of this may sound easy; often it is not. In a highly complicated or technical case, it is extremely difficult. Making some cases interesting and understandable truly separates the great lawyers from others.

There are two tools, in particular, that a lawyer must use to remain persuasive, interesting, and understandable while telling your story. First, you must develop **themes** and a **theory of the case**. You learned about these while enjoying all of your favorite fairy tales. When a great storyteller is done, the audience remembers certain key themes that were developed, regularly and consistently, throughout the story, and the audience ends up understanding the basic message or moral that the story was intended to convey. Just as with a good book, where this process appears effortless to the reader, it is actually the result of painstaking planning and organization on the part of the author, a process that begins well before the first sentence of the story is written.

A second critical tool of storytelling is **visualization**. Not only do people learn and remember far more from what they see than from what they hear (I won't bore you with all of the statistics and scientific studies on this point), but they are also far more interested and entertained when they are visually stimulated. Visualization is both using your storytelling to create visual images in the mind's eye of the audience, as well as using actual illustrations or visual imagery. Your favorite fairy tale books were filled with both; phrases that created clear, stark images in your mind (sometimes beautiful, sometimes frightening) of that forest, of the witch, of the beautiful castle—along with beautiful illustrations on every second or third page, illustrations that kept you moving through the story and that helped you visualize the entire tale.

As you will see, your story is told far more effectively with the proper use of these tools: themes, a theory of the case, and visualizations, used effectively and consistently not only in your lawyer's arguments to the jury, but in the questions asked by your lawyer of the witnesses; along with the careful use of graphics and visual evidence to make the presentation clear, interesting, and move the audience through the pages without becoming confused, and without falling asleep.

It's Usually About Money

Too often, people go into a lawsuit seeking revenge, vindication, or some other all-too-human emotional reward which is largely unavailable in our system of justice. Most cases are about money, and in most cases, all that will be obtained at the end of the case is winning or losing money. No matter how outraged, hurt, or offended you may be by the facts that led to your dispute, you need to face the reality of what this litigation process can do for you, and what it cannot. This may be one of the first things you want to talk to your lawyer about.

About Judges And Juries

The conventional wisdom is that judges approach cases more logically than juries do, but I have found that this is not always the case. Judges have seen more cases, and are somewhat trained in logical thinking, but they bring the same human foibles to the process of making a decision that we all do.

It is indeed an interesting process, watching a group of ordinary citizens deciding your fate, and judging what did and did not happen, who is right, and who is wrong. Three things help the jury system work fairly well. First, we have a basic trust in the concept that a group of citizens will at least try to be fair, and there is less concern about corruption, influence, or that decisions will be "fixed" by politics or power. Second, jurors operate as a group, and what one juror does not grasp, remember, or connect with can be compensated for by other jurors who are there, in the jury room, to remind and explain during their deliberations. Finally, the fact is that jurors, almost always, take their role very, very seriously, and do their very best to get it right.

Now the bad news. Jurors are human beings. Human beings, in turn, are typically ill-equipped to come to conclusions that are purely rational and logical about a series of facts that are presented to them. Numerous social science studies show that our brains are very good at many things, but they are not particularly good at that. We usually believe that we are processing information reasonably, and using logic to come to our opinions and conclusions. Often, that is not what we are doing at all. We approach most information with a whole battery of preconceptions, assumptions, and prejudices, often unknowingly. Some people will almost <u>always</u> believe a police officer, and some people will almost <u>never</u> believe a police officer. The facts, or that individual police officer's character, don't matter. We tend to relate to and empathize with people who we think are like us, or with people who are in situations that remind us of things that have touched our lives, for good or for bad. Any parent knows that you respond differently to issues concerning children, after you have children. If you have known people with mental illness, if you have been injured, if you suffered injustice, or if you live in a sheltered and privileged environment, that past history will all have a significant impact on your thinking as you sit in judgment of other people's life experiences.

All of what I have just said can be summarized simply: Depending upon what your dispute is about and who you are, there are some jurors who will be great for you, and some who will be terrible for you. There is a general belief that great trial lawyers are good at picking juries. Actually, lawyers don't pick juries at all. They "unpick" juries. You don't get to decide who will be on your jury panel. What you do get to do is to look at who is on your jury panel, and throw out a few of the ones that scare you the most. Depending upon who you are and what your story is, certain people will be <u>exactly</u> who you do <u>not</u> want to be deciding your case. Unfortunately, the truth is that there is no reliable and consistent way to figure out who those people are. It is true that experienced trial lawyers, and professional jury consultants, can do a good job of guessing intelligently, and can improve your odds. At the end of the day, however, jury selection still has to rely on instinct, and even the best only get it right some of the time.

The most dangerous juror is a juror who is likely not to like you or your story, and who is likely to play an important role in the jury deliberations because of the force of that juror's personality or for some other reason. When a jury begins its deliberations, some of the jurors will be leaders, and some of them will be passive and fol-low the crowd. A "bad" juror for you who is passive is less dangerous, but one who is a leader is poison. The leader-ship quality can come from a variety of directions. Some people have very strong personalities, or will be naturally looked upon by other jurors as more knowledgeable and someone to be deferred to. Other jurors will fight for attention and a leadership role, simply because, in the rest of their life, they feel powerless or unimportant, and this is their one chance at being important. Other factors can come to play, as well. I once had a trial where a potential juror disclosed that she was a secretary. Neither I, nor my opposing counsel, thought to ask her whether she knew how to take shorthand (few people do this anymore). She did, sat on the jury, shorthanded the entire trial, and literally walked into the jury room with her own word-by-word transcript of the trial. Obviously, she now had a position of power and influence in those deliberations far beyond what we might have anticipated. All of the jurors would be asking her what exactly was said about this and that. Good thing she liked us.

Why Are There So Many Lawsuits

Do you find it interesting that we, one of the most progressive and free societies in the world, are the most litigious? Perhaps it is not entirely a coincidence. The role of courts in a civilized society is to provide a system that allows people to resolve their human disputes in a civilized way. In the old days, there were not nearly as many lawsuits. When people had an argument, they just beat each other up or killed each other. The Hatfields and the McCoys. Alexander Hamilton and Aaron Burr. But wouldn't it have been wonderful if Hamilton and Burr had engaged in a "trial of the century," rather than in the senseless slaughter of one of our great founding fathers. Our legal system and our society do, in many ways, almost encourage litigation. It may well be true that, in some instances, they encourage a dispute that, otherwise, simply would not have occurred. But the underlying message of the American legal system is this: if you have a dispute with someone, bring it to the big white building downtown. We will help you resolve it in a civilized way. At least in a relatively civilized way.

What Is The "Adversary System"

Most people don't probably think about this very much, but there is one critical assumption in our legal system. The assumption is that the best way to find the truth in a dispute between two people is to have each person represented by a professional storyteller, who helps them tell their side of the story to a neutral judge or jury deciding who is right. This is called the adversary system. This is why your lawyer is not trying to be fair, neutral, or decide what is right. Your lawyer is 100% on your side, and will do nothing more than try to tell your side of the story as forcefully and persuasively as possible, whether you are right or completely wrong. There is a confusing aspect to this role-playing which causes many people to think that all lawyers are dishonest. How can you represent a guilty person? How can you represent someone if you know that they are wrong? The answer to those questions is found in the underlying key assumption of our entire system of justice. Each side has a lawyer, and the lawyer is not pretending to be the judge. If each lawyer does his job well, the judge and jury will be in the best position to come to a conclusion as to the truth, and to a just outcome. If you can think of a better system, write your Congressman.

Chapter 3

How to Pick a Lawyer

There is no one answer to this question that can cover every situation, because your priorities will be different depending upon whether you are suing or being sued, whether the matter is civil or criminal, whether it is simple or complicated, whether it is personal or business. However, there are some general considerations that almost always apply.

First, you must understand that, from your side of the table, this is likely to be a very personal relationship. You are taking a problem that is very important to you, and putting it in the hands of this lawyer. This is not just another case to you. You must really trust this person, and you will feel very dependent upon him to take good care of you. In this respect, the relationship is not very different from the relationship you have with your doctor.

Unfortunately, like your doctor, the lawyer may not always see things in exactly the same way. In the reality of modern medicine, many of us find ourselves depending upon doctors who barely know us, and barely remember us, because they have so many patients and because they are limited in the time that they can spend with each patient. In the same way, the modern lawyer often has many cases and many clients that are being juggled, and unless your case is a very big one or you are a regular client, you may at times be frustrated by the difficulty you experience in getting the lawyer's attention to your matter. You may occasionally feel like another number in the waiting room. The lawyer has a very serious responsibility to do all that is possible to avoid those frustrations on your part, but there are practical pressures on the lawyer as well. If the lawyer is working on a contingency, then the lawyer has pressure to be as efficient as possible in the use of his time, and not to spend a lot of time socializing or just talking to you without purpose. The pressure is to get to the point of what has to be discussed. Similarly, if the lawyer is billing you by the hour, you don't want to pay for anymore of this lawyer's time than necessary to get the job done, and the lawyer doesn't want to give away a lot of time either.

As a result of all of these factors, each lawyer and client must work out a relationship that works for them, balancing the very personal nature of the relationship with the need to use time efficiently, and balancing the client's need for personal attention with the business practicalities of the situation. Your perspective may range from vulnerability and dependence, to a sense that you are the customer paying a lot of money and deserving to get good service. The bottom line is that your needs must be met, whatever they are, and how best to make that happen will be discussed in the next chapter on managing your lawyer.

Once you understand the basic relationship, you can begin the process of selecting an attorney. This process will be different in different situations, but the following points will apply in most instances. First, you should probably speak with several lawyers before hiring one. You can select your candidates from personal references given to you by people you know and trust, by researching which lawyers have been identified as knowledgeable in your community concerning the particular problem you have, or even by contacting your local bar association. Good references are important, but you can't rely too much upon them. You have to come to your own conclusions about whether this is the right lawyer for you, and that is not an easy process. You should find out about the lawyer's background, including education and prior professional experience. You can also ask the lawyer for personal references from existing or prior clients. If you have a rock-solid reference from someone you really trust, you may go with that alone. In most instances, you will have to rely a good deal on your impressions of the lawyer after conducting an initial interview.

You should almost never have to pay for an initial interview with a lawyer. You should be prepared to explain, in a few minutes, the basic nature of the lawsuit you are facing. Always tell the lawyer the complete truth; this is very important in order to get a valid read and useful advice. Listen very carefully to the lawyer's reaction to your case, and then ask clear and hard questions about the issues that matter to you most. They should include: If I hire you, who will actually handle my case; will other lawyers work on the case with you? What are your rates, and what is this likely to cost me? Based upon what I have told you about my case, what do you think of it, and, what do you think my chances are? What should I expect in this lawsuit, in terms of how much time it will last, and what will happen? What are the biggest problems that you see with my case? What would you do if you were me?

Listen very carefully to the answers, and observe the lawyer carefully as well. How do you feel about the answers that you are receiving? Is the lawyer really listening to you, and really understanding what you are saying? Does the lawyer appear to care sincerely about your problem? Is the lawyer evasive in ways that make you uncomfortable?

What the lawyer says to you should make sense. If the lawyer can't explain to you where your case is headed, in a way that is clearly understandable to you, then you should question whether this lawyer can explain your case to someone else. This is also a time to really trust your instincts. This is like a first date. If you feel that it is going well, then it may be appropriate to place your trust in this lawyer. If you have a bad feeling, interview another lawyer.

One thing to avoid, if at all possible, is developing an adversary relationship with your own lawyer. You have to come to a reasonable agreement about fees and costs, and how your case will be taken care of. On the other hand, if your relationship starts out as a hard negotiation, followed by constant bickering about bills and activity, you are getting into a relationship that may be harmful to your case. The best relationship with a lawyer is where that lawyer is really on your side, not arguing with you. If you find yourself arguing with your lawyer excessively, it may be time to think seriously about changing lawyers.

A final and obvious point—women become great trial lawyers just as easily as men do, and many of my best colleagues and adversaries have been women. I say this only because this book will refer to lawyers with the masculine pronoun "he," solely for ease of presentation (avoiding he/she, etc.)

Chapter 4

How to Manage Your Lawyer

Once you have hired a lawyer, you must manage this relationship, and manage how your case is being handled. Again, like the doctor/patient relationship, where the patient must take ultimate responsibility for his or her health, you must make sure that you are being taken care of properly. This means at least two things: You must be **comfortable** that your case is being handled properly, and you must remain **informed** about what is going on with your case.

Your goal is to develop a relationship of trust. You want to get to the point where you can let the lawyer do his job, get the feedback you need, and get on with your life. This lawsuit is probably going to last for several months or even several years, and the best thing for you is not to be consumed by it on a daily basis. Once you have given the lawyer the information needed and made initial tactical decisions, as will be discussed later, the best thing for you is to put the lawsuit in the hands of the lawyer, and be involved only as needed and when needed. Developing a good relationship of trust with the lawyer will also have other benefits. It will be easier to find the balance that you must find between a real need for information, versus general anxiety on your part concerning the case. Finding that balance is important, not only for your own state of mind, but also in terms of cost. Once you and your lawyer get on a good track, you want to spend the time together that you need to spend, whether in person or by phone, but not more. Time is money.

So how do you manage this relationship and manage the lawyer's work?

Managing With the "Why?" Question

This single word can be a disarmingly effective management tool. Careful use (but not abuse) of the "**why?**" question is a critical method for you to manage this entire problem. Do we have a significant problem in this case? **Why?** Do you think this case will go to trial? **Why?** Should we be aggressive from the beginning in initiating discovery? **Why?** What is our strategy in this case? **Why?** What will this case cost? **Why?**

Your lawyer should have answers to these questions that are thoughtful and make sense. This does not mean that your lawyer is likely to have a <u>certain</u> answer to any of these questions. An honest lawyer cannot guarantee you the outcome of your case, nor what it will cost, nor what the other side is going to do. But the lawyer should be able to give you answers that show that he is thinking about your case seriously, understands it, and has a plan. Proper use of the **why?** question as a management tool will get you the answers that you need, and force a discussion between you and your lawyer that will get you on the same page about where you are going with your lawsuit. Like any good tool, don't abuse it.

Remember again that the goal in your relationship is to get to the point where you can let the lawyer do his job, involving you as needed for information or decisions, and allowing you to get along with your life while this lawsuit proceeds. If the relationship is not going in that direction, it may be time to seriously consider changing lawyers, although this is a very serious decision, and must be made carefully. One of the key factors you are assessing, as you manage with the why? question is whether your lawyer has a strategy, whether your lawyer is acting or just reacting, whether there is a plan and direction to your lawsuit.

Bad Signs

There are red flags that you must be on the lookout for, and that can signal a problem with your lawyer relationship. First, the lawyer should be able to answer your questions, and the answers should make sense to you. If your lawyer is unresponsive, doesn't want to talk to you, or gives you answers that you don't understand, this is a bad sign. Another bad sign is surprises; unavoidable surprises are a part of litigation, and the lawyer can't control everything that the judge or the lawyer on the other side is going to do. But if you see a pattern where the lawyer gets you to expect one thing and then something else happens, this may be a bad sign. If the lawyer makes a significant change to his analysis of the case, or his assessment of your chances of winning the case, without being able to point to you some clear change in the evidence, or something new and that could not have been known before that causes this change in opinion, then you should be concerned. If your lawyer appears unprepared for hearings or for activity in the lawsuit, and is doing too much for your case at the last minute, this is also a reason for concern. If your lawyer is late to meetings or court appearances, this is definitely bad. If your lawyer appears disorganized, or is not clear on what the court rules are that apply to your case, this is a bad sign as well. Finally, if your lawyer doesn't seem to remember the key facts of your dispute, or the contents of the important documents, that is a problem.

Again, be reasonable in what you expect from your lawyer. The best lawyers will be surprised, even flabbergasted, by what judges will do in cases. The best lawyer cannot control everything that the lawyer on the other side does. Your lawyer cannot protect you from being inconvenienced by activity in the lawsuit, including depositions (where your testimony is given under oath before the case goes to trial), written discovery (where you have to answer written questions, under oath), document productions (where you have to give up all of your documents which are relevant to the lawsuit), etc. All of these activities in connection with your lawsuit also have court-imposed deadlines, which again, your lawyer can't necessarily change. Avoid, to the greatest degree possible, getting into an adversarial relationship with your lawyer. This process may well be very stressful to you, and there will be times when you get very frustrated. Letting off a little steam is okay, but keep your lawyer on your side. If you are having serious difficulties doing that, you may not have the right lawyer.

Chapter 5

How To Manage Your Emotions During A Lawsuit

If you are in a lawsuit and are very emotional or stressed out about it, it is critical that you face up to this fact and deal with it. This is true for several reasons. First, you will make bad decisions in the lawsuit, and will harm your chances of "winning." Second, you may start expecting your lawyer to solve your emotional issues, which is not what a lawyer is equipped to do. Finally, in your determination to fight the good fight, you may ignore a need to get real help when you really need it.

Take stock of your emotions, both at the beginning and throughout the process. Moments of anger or frustration are, of course, an inevitable part of being in a dispute—just don't make decisions while you are emotional. But if you are not sleeping at night, if you are consumed with anger, fear, depression, or anxiety, then it is critical that you face this fact as a separate problem from the lawsuit itself. First, understand that your feelings are both normal and appropriate—lawsuits are often about very important and/or very upsetting things. The problems are real and so are your reactions to them. Next, understand that, both to survive your lawsuit and to win it, you must treat your emotional needs properly.

When emotional needs are ignored, litigants lose control, often with bad consequences. Sometimes they lash out irrationally at their lawyers, or change lawyers without a good reason to do so. A combative relationship with your own lawyer, or changing lawyers impulsively, can really, really hurt your case. So can making decisions about settling or not settling your case out of fear. Becoming obsessed or paranoid about what the other side is doing is another standard war injury. A good lawyer on the other side can smell these fears and anxieties, and knows how to capitalize on them.

I firmly believe that your lawyer must accept responsibility for identifying these problems, and for doing all the lawyer can to address them. There is a great deal the lawyer can and must do, primarily by explaining to you what is going on, answering your questions, guiding your decisions, and gaining your confidence that the case is well under control. Communication is the key. However, your lawyer is not a therapist, and not trained, nor there to provide you with emotional support past a reasonable point. Depending upon what other support systems you have, and depending upon your needs, you must consider whether other professional help is required. There is nothing wrong, and everything smart and right, with getting therapy or other help when you are in a period of great stress in your life, especially if the stress is impacting on your ability to function.

Finally, "winning" aside, ignoring your physical or mental health while you fight your case makes no sense.

The goal of this lawsuit is to make your life better or to keep what your have, right? No one would pick a doctor who would kill the patient to cure the disease. Put things in perspective. Whether you come out a "winner" will be a function of how you, as a whole person, come out of this process. Take care of yourself.

Chapter 6

What Are Arbitration And Mediation; How Are They Different?

Arbitration and mediation are sometimes referred to collectively as Alternative Dispute Resolution or ADR. What they have in common is taking your dispute outside the court system to resolve it. However, people sometimes confuse these two processes, and they are completely different.

Arbitration is trial by private judge. The typical format is that one arbitrator, or a panel of three, decide your case. They are paid to do this. There is usually no right of appeal, no jury, and the rules of law and evidence are not usually followed as closely as they would be in a court. The decision is final, and the judgment is enforceable in the same way as it would be if it were a court judgment. Cases are decided by arbitration, usually, because the parties have agreed to this process, or because the contract or controlling document that they are arguing about has an "arbitration clause" requiring that any disputes be resolved this way. Arbitrators often, but not always, work for large arbitration associations, like the American Arbitration Association or various private judging companies.

If you are given a choice between arbitration or staying in the court system, then you must carefully review with your lawyer all of the costs and benefits of each alternative as it applies to you. Arbitration is often, but not always, faster and cheaper. Arbitration awards are often, but not always, in smaller dollar amounts than what a jury might award. Arbitrators are sometimes, but definitely not always, more logical or rational in reviewing the facts of a case than a jury might be. Arbitrators are sometimes, but not always, less tied to narrow points of law than a judge might be. In an arbitration, there will usually, but not always, be much less pretrial "discovery"—the taking of depositions, exchanging of documents, and asking of written questions under oath. As you can see, there is no simple answer as to whether arbitration will be better for you, in your case. There are many factors to consider, and your lawyer must guide you.

Mediation is a voluntary process where the parties try to negotiate a settlement with the help of a professional, neutral negotiator. It can occur before a lawsuit is filed, or before the case goes to trial. Mediation is a settlement process, not a decision-making process. The mediator is given no power to decide anything, but is instead a middle person through whom both sides talk to each other. It is a very specific skill, and a good mediator will increase significantly the chances that a negotiation will result in a successful settlement. Some mediators are retired judges, and some are lawyers or other professionals trained in the art of mediation. Some retired judges are good mediators, and some are poor mediators. If the retired judge does not understand that mediating is a totally different role, and continues to try to act like a judge during the process, he or she will usually wind up doing a lousy job.

A good mediator is a "dishonest broker," which does not mean that he is trying to cheat you. At the end of a successful mediation, the case has settled. Usually, both sides walk away thinking that the mediator liked them better, believed them more, and was trying to help them. In truth, he or she is neutral, and is simply trying to bring the parties together.

There are many different styles of mediation, and different ways that mediators run the process. Here is a typical mediation procedure: The mediator begins with all parties and their lawyers in the room. It is critical to any mediation that the people involved in the lawsuit be present, along with their lawyers. The mediator begins by explaining the mediation process, and what will be happening during the course of the day. Then, each side is given the opportunity to tell their side of the story, without confronting each other, so that each side can hear what the other has to say. After that, the parties are separated, usually for the rest of the process. You and your lawyer are in one room, and the other side is in a different room. The mediator begins "shuttle diplomacy" between the two rooms. The mediator has explained to both sides that he will keep in strict confidence anything that is told to him in confidence, but will disclose what he is told to disclose. You and your lawyer spend the rest of your time talking only to the mediator, not to the other side. This allows the negotiation process to proceed without anger, and also facilitates a candid conversation about the strengths and weaknesses of your case, with someone you are not angry at. If the process works, everyone starts letting their hair down, and the mediator finds a point where everyone can meet.

In many jurisdictions, the judge will at some point require the parties to at least attempt mediation, before the case goes to trial. Whether or not this happens, you should discuss with your lawyer whether, and when, mediation would be a good idea. A good lawyer will tell you that the mediation process is surprisingly successful, surprisingly often, even in very emotional or difficult cases. A skilled mediator is experienced at dealing with parties who start out very far apart in their expectations, and who may even hate each other. An experienced mediator knows how to control and engage the parties in a constructive direction, so that, while acting only in their own self-interest, they move closer together. A widely respected mediator whom I used on many occasions, and who was himself a prominent retired appellate justice, used to begin each mediation by telling both sides that the litigation process is a machine whereby you enter as a pig and you exit as a sausage. The greatest benefit of resolving your case by mediation and settlement is that you control the process. No matter how violent your disagreement is with the other side, if the two of you pick a solution, it will be an outcome that you can at least live with. You will probably both be unhappy with the result; neither one of you got everything that you wanted, often far from it. But if you put the outcome in the hands of strangers, they may hand you a result that makes everyone miserable, and at great cost. You have no control over what a judge or a jury will do with your case, and the result can at times be astonishing, even to the best and most experienced lawyers. There is often a very good reason to try, early in the dispute, to save a great deal of money and time by pursuing a settlement early, and mediation is often the best way to accomplish this. However, whether any of this applies to you and your case depends on many things, and you must rely upon your lawyer to guide you. Remember, again, that most cases are about money, and in most cases, money is the only thing that can be obtained by either side at the end of the matter. Seeking revenge or vindication is usually a bad reason to continue a lawsuit.

Chapter 7

What Is "Winning"?

You have undoubtedly heard stories about lawyers who "win" all of their cases. What exactly does that mean? The answer is that it may not mean much at all. For example, some lawyers only handle car accident cases. A smart plaintiff's lawyer who handles car accident cases will make sure to settle any case where there is any question at all about who was at fault. The only cases that he will take to trial are cases where liability is clear, and the only question is "how much." If you try 50 cases where your client was rear-ended on the freeway, you don't have to be Clarence Darrow to win all of them. But what is a "win"?

Suppose that in one of those cases, the injuries are very serious, and the real value of the case is $500,000. However, the plaintiff's lawyer has not prepared the case properly, has not effectively explained to the jury his client's damages, and has not properly prepared his medical experts. As a result, the defense lawyer succeeds in confusing the plaintiff's medical experts in front of the jury, and lowering the jury's view of damages. Suppose further that, as a result of all of this, the jury awards the plaintiff $100,000. Who won? The plaintiff's lawyer can say that he "won" the case, but it is really the defense lawyer that turned a $500,000 liability into a $100,000 verdict. Great job.

In a different scenario, suppose the lawyer is representing you in a complicated business contract dispute. The other side offers to settle with you for $200,000. Your lawyer tells you to turn that settlement down, because your case is worth a million dollars. You pay the lawyer $250,000 to litigate the case through trial. The jury gives you $75,000 as an award. Did you win?

When people talk about lawsuits, the discussion is always about winning. The media tells you how often famous lawyers win their cases. Both the media and the entertainment industry project lawsuits as being about winning, where winning is easily defined (in other words, not really defined at all),and winners are heroes. Neither the media nor the entertainment industry spends much effort provoking any thought about what the concept of winning really is. In truth, if a lawyer charges you $100,000 to solve a $50,000 problem, you have lost. In truth, if you pass up the opportunity to make a deal which would leave you better off, you have lost. In truth, many of the best lawyers in the country handle primarily very, very difficult cases; they technically "lose" many of those cases—but if you dig down deep, you will find that they got **great** results for their client under the circumstances.

If you want to win your lawsuit, the first thing you have to understand clearly is what "winning" means.

The Definition of Winning

Litigation is a problem-solving function. The lawyer is handed a series of cards (the facts, the evidence, and the witnesses) that cannot for the most part be changed. The goal (winning) is to play those cards to the best possible result. Results are measured by outcome and cost.

Let's examine each sentence in this definition. First, remember that your lawsuit is simply a problem that you are trying to solve. You need to define clearly what your realistic goals in the lawsuit are; this will provide your framework for preparing for and fighting the case, as well as your framework for assessing how well you are doing. This is why we talked early on about the fact that most lawsuits are about money, as well as about the importance of separating your anger and emotions from your analysis. Most people who think their goal is "revenge" never feel that they got what they were looking for, and quickly lose any sense of how to measure how they are doing. Defining what the "problem" is in your lawsuit is often an easy task, but sometimes it is less obvious or simply defined. Take the time to think through what the problem is. For example, an employer with many employees, facing a lawsuit that he believes to be unjust, may define the problem beyond the individual dispute. If this employee wins at trial or gets a settlement, it may encourage other employees to bring similar lawsuits. As another example, if you are suing someone because they damaged your reputation by publishing embarrassing but untrue allegations concerning your personal life, money alone may not solve your problem. You need your reputation back, too.

Next, you must understand that your lawyer cannot win this case simply by being a "great lawyer." This is why we discussed, at the beginning, the fact that a trial is a story, and that your lawyer will tell this story with witnesses, documents, and other evidence. Your story will often only be a good as your weakest storyteller, irrespective of what "actually happened." In order to define what a "win" in your case will be, you have to understand carefully what cards you have given your lawyer, and assess realistically how good those cards are. This requires you, as the client, with the help of your lawyer, to engage in what is perhaps the most difficult process for any person involved in a lawsuit: you have to separate what you believe the facts are, from what those facts will appear to be based upon the actual evidence that the jury will hear and see.

Next, you can begin to develop a picture of what a "win" will be in your case. It is critical to do this, because it is only by doing this that you can make good decisions about what your settlement position will be prior to trial, and it is also only by doing this that you will be able to make good decisions about how to handle your case and how much to invest in it. Equally important, remember that in a lawsuit, every evaluation is subject to change. You must remain flexible, and be prepared to change your evaluation when the factors that support that evaluation change. Changes can be dramatic, such as the death of a witness before trial or the discovery of a document that changes the picture of what happened; it can also be subtle, such as discovering that a key witness does not project himself or his part of the story as well as had been hoped.

Winning for some criminal defendants is simply avoiding execution. Winning for some companies is simply having a company left when the lawsuit is over. Winning in a divorce may be no more than protecting the children from as much pain as possible. Winning for an injured child may mean not only cash today, but a structure to take care of her medical bills and other needs for the rest of the child's life. Winning in a business dispute may mean not only solving the current argument, but leaving the door open for the parties to do more business in the future. Winning for a manufacturer or drug company may be restoring the confidence of the public that its product is safe, and that consumer safety is more important to it than profits.

Finally, results are indeed measured by both outcome and cost. You don't want to cure the disease by killing the patient, you don't want to solve a little problem by creating a big problem, and you have to assess all of the costs, both tangible and intangible, that come with your result, in order to determine whether that result is really a "win." Too often, lawsuits are driven by such animosity that the parties wind up on a course of mutually assured destruction, testing which one will be the first to go bankrupt or expire. Most often, both lose in this kind of battle.

There is a wonderful story about two men in a small village, who had long despised each other bitterly. One day, an angel came to the first man and made him an offer. The angel told the man that he would give him anything he wanted, anything at all, and in any quantity he desired. The only condition of the gift, said the angel, is that, whatever I give to you, I will give double to this other man that you hate. This condition made the first man agonize deeply, for there was so much that he wanted, so many things that he could ask for; but he could not bear that his enemy would receive the same thing twice over. He tormented himself pondering this decision for some time. Suddenly, a great smile came to his face. "I've got it," he said. "I know what I want." The angel asked him for his wish. "Pluck out one of my eyes," the man replied.

Chapter 8

How Good Is Your Case: The Initial Assessment

It is important to examine this question seriously, from the very beginning of the dispute. Do your best to begin an initial assessment of your lawsuit before you take any steps, including selecting your lawyer. Once you have a lawyer, he will help you to develop that assessment, and working together on this is a critical stage in the development of your working relationship together. This is a good time to begin managing your lawyer with the "why?" question, getting your questions answered, and getting on the same page with your lawyer about where the case is going.

Two things are important to keep in mind as you begin an **initial** assessment of your case. First, this is an initial assessment. As important as it is to come to opinions now about the strength of your case, it is equally important to understand that, frequently, the assessment of a case must change as events unfold in the lawsuit. This may seem illogical at first, because, after all, what happened to start this dispute has all taken place already, and those facts are not going to change. So why would the evaluation of the case change? The answer is that a trial is a story, and what matters is how that story will unfold during the trial. Very little about the facts is likely to change, but you will know much more, later on, about the quality of the evidence and the witnesses, on **both** sides, than you do now. This additional, and critical, information will be developed during the discovery and investigation phase, as will be discussed later, and will support a far more detailed analytical framework for a final assessment of your lawsuit, incorporating all of the critical facts that you will learn during the lawsuit about how the trial is likely to go.

In addition to remembering that this is an initial assessment which is subject to change, the second important factor to remember is that, in order to assess how good **your** case is, you must assess **the** case. This means that, as difficult as this may sometimes be, you must evaluate the case by looking **at** both sides and **from** both sides. Looking **at** both sides of the case means looking not only at the story you are going to tell, but at the story they are going to tell, and at the witnesses they are going to present, and at the documents they are going to present. Looking at the case **from** both sides means putting yourself in your adversary's shoes; trying to understand his motivations, his emotional reaction to the dispute, and his point of view. All of this is critical in order to estimate how a judge or jury will view the case after hearing both sides.

With all of this in mind, you are ready to begin developing your initial assessment.

The First Questions to Ask Yourself

For a lawyer, unfolding the initial storyline and cast of characters in a new lawsuit can actually be one of the most exciting parts of the process. One of the things that I love about being a lawyer is that every case is different, with its own cast of characters, dramatic story, intellectual challenges, and details to absorb. To me, that new file and those new boxes of documents are like Christmas presents that I get to open, revealing a brand new human drama, new mysteries to solve, and new areas of knowledge to explore. If you have a bit of the "Renaissance" personality, this can really be fun. I have learned so much, through the years, about science, technology, medicine, accounting, and virtually every other field of study—all through lawsuits.

For the client, of course, it's not usually as much fun. However, this is the time to focus on what will be important about this case.

- What is the general storyline of this dispute? What happened? Where? And to whom? What parts of this story are easy to understand and what parts of this story are hard to understand? Are there parts of this story that are going to resonate with the jury emotionally?

- Who are the likely witnesses if this case goes to trial? Where are those witnesses now? Which of these witnesses are likely to help, or hurt, your side of the story? Do you have any serious witness problems, such as bad storytellers, or reluctant storytellers?

- What are the key documents in this case? Where are those documents? Do you have all of those documents? Will you be able to get all of the documents that you don't have? Don't forget electronic records.

- Who are the key players in this drama? Who are the decision-makers on both sides of the case, including key decision-makers in corporations, partnerships, or insurance companies? Who are the lawyers, and who will be the judge?

- What are likely to be the central legal issues in the case? Are the legal issues in this case simple, or complicated? Is the law established and clear concerning the legal issues in this lawsuit, or are there issues that are not so clear? Is this the kind of case that could wind up having to be decided by a court of appeal?

- Are there likely to be any significant evidentiary disputes? Are there key documents that may be subject to challenge as to whether they will get admitted into evidence and before the jury? Is there any key testimony from any witness that may be subject to an argument that it should be excluded from evidence?

- Are there any sensitive political issues, public relations issues, publicity issues, or other similar factors involved in this lawsuit? Is there any potential for criminal liability? Are there any individuals whose career, employment, or compensation may be impacted by how this lawsuit develops? Are any of the witnesses going to be pointing fingers at each other, or concerned about blame?

In examining these questions, some of the information will come primarily from the client, some primarily from the lawyer, and much of it will be developed as a process of information-sharing and communication between the client and the lawyer. Both lawyer and client must get a handle on the storyline, carefully review all of the documents that are available, think through the cast of characters, and think through all of the issues that may need to be dealt with immediately.

There are three things to focus on as you begin to develop your initial assessment. First, are there any damage control issues here? Is there something taking place right now that you should stop, or is there something that you should be doing immediately to improve your position? For example, if you are accused of harming someone's reputation, or someone's credit, or someone's financial condition, you may want to look immediately at whether there are steps you should be taking to minimize your risk. If you are being sued by someone who fell down your broken stairs, you had better not only think through your lawsuit, but fix those stairs. If you are bringing a claim because you lost your job, or because you were injured, you must make sure that you are taking reasonable steps to find a new job or get appropriate medical care; otherwise, the other side will claim that your damages are mostly your fault, not theirs.

The second thing to focus on, based upon your initial review, is whether you want to move immediately to exploring early settlement, including by way of mediation. Is this is the kind of case that will be more easily settled now, rather than later? Is the other side looking for a quick resolution, or for revenge? Is it in your best interest to settle the case now, rather than later? Will your case become stronger when all of the evidence and all of the documents are revealed? Or worse? Based upon all of this, what should the tone be of the initial contact made by you or your lawyer with the opposing parties and their counsel? This last question is critical, and often badly handled by poor lawyering or a failure to control emotion. Sometimes you want to be very aggressive and hardnosed in your initial contacts with the other side. Sometimes you want to be conciliatory. Sometimes you want to be ambiguous and see where they are coming from. A lawyer that approaches every case with a cookie cutter is a lousy lawyer. The initial assessment that you make of both your side of the case and the other side of the case should lead you to a thoughtful approach about how to make initial contact with the other side.

Finally, your initial assessment is the foundation for developing your **Strategic Plan** for the litigation. It also leads to the development of your **themes** and your **theory of the case**. More on these items later.

Your initial assessment will also allow you to outline one of the most important things you need to make a list of at the beginning of the case. What you **don't** know at this point, what documents you don't have at this point, and what factual or legal questions you can't answer until more work has been done.

A Structure For The Initial Assessment —How To "Grade" The Facts Of Your Case

The outcome of your case may turn, in part or in whole, on legal issues. Your lawyer will explain to you what legal issues arise from your case, and how they will impact your case. Cases turn on legal issues and factual issues. In a jury trial, the judge will instruct the jury as to the law, as it applies to your case. The jury will decide what the facts were, and then, applying the law as explained by the judge, render a verdict.

In forming your initial assessment of the facts, try "grading" the basic storyline, the witnesses, and the documents.

What Type Of Case Is This?

Type "A"

The defendant faces a case that is not defensible. It messed up badly, and it knows it. The only question in the case is how much the plaintiff will recover. There is no question about liability, and there is no question about the existence of real damages.

Type "B"
There are two sides to this story. Liability and damages are both unclear.

Type "C"
Liability could be a real problem for the defendant, but the plaintiff does not seem to have any damages. No harm, no foul?

Type "D"
Liability appears to be remote, but the damages could be significant. The defendant doesn't "think" that it did anything really wrong, but the plaintiff has had a very bad outcome, and so the defendant is worried anyway.

Type "E"
The plaintiff's case is completely without merit, and this is a frivolous lawsuit.

What Kind of Witnesses Do We Have?

1. The plaintiff is (a) very sympathetic; (b) a convicted felon; (c) all of the above.

2. The defendant is (a) very sympathetic; (b) very unsympathetic; (c) a large corporation; (d) a convicted felon; (e) a lawyer.

3. Third party witnesses are (a) credible and very damaging; (b) credible and very helpful; (c) not very credible, but if believed, damaging; (d) not very credible, but if believed, helpful.

4. The other side's witnesses are (a) credible and very damaging; (b) credible and very helpful; (c) not very credible, but if believed, damaging; (d) not very credible, but if believed, helpful.

Our Witnesses

Remember if this case goes to trial, someone has to tell your story. **Your story may be as good as your weakest storyteller.** Another key factor about your witnesses: they have to be available. I can't tell you how many times I've represented a company in a case where they had several employees who were great witnesses and supported their side of the story completely. Unfortunately, before trial, some of those employees were fired, or otherwise left their job with bad feelings. Now, these great witnesses were either unavailable or no longer on our side.

I once had an emotionally charged case involving the termination of a high-level employee. It was a case punctuated by hot-button issues and very serious charges on both sides. Although there were some difficult facts and some bad evidence, my client was absolutely convinced that firing this person had not only been justifiable, but was in fact the right and necessary thing to do. I was equally convinced of that conclusion. Because of how the story unfolded and the decision was made, there was only one possible choice as the key storyteller for our side, to explain why this person was fired and in fact <u>had</u> to be fired. That storyteller was the human resources manager, a very bright, articulate, and credible witness. Only one problem. Right before the case went to trial, she left the company under difficult circumstances, totally unrelated to this case, and filed <u>her own</u> wrongful termination lawsuit! We now had a completely different case. The facts were the same, as were the merits. But the trial was going to be different.

What Kind Of Documents Do We Have?

Carefully review all of the documents that are available, and assess how they will play out in terms of the story. Don't make the mistake of falling in love with the documents that help your side of the case, and glossing over the other ones. Focus first on the documents that can be used against you, and on how they could best be used against you. That is what the other side is going to do, so you might as well get used to it. Next, identify what documents you do not have, where they are, and whether you can get them. Finally, by all means do not forget email and electronic records. In many cases today, most or all of the key documents are electronic. Moreover, it is simply amazing what stupid things people will say in emails, and how they just cannot get it through their heads that when they hit "delete," the email is often still there to be found. This factor may be a tremendous advantage for you, or a tremendous risk; assess both. If there are bad documents on your side of the case, you want to find them before the other side does, and before the other side asks for them. The initial assessment of documents helps you formulate your strategic plan for investigating the case further and for doing discovery against the other side. Also, remind your lawyer, in case he forgets, that documents are only useful at trial if they are **admissible**. This means that, under the rules of evidence, there is a sufficient foundation and basis to let the jury see them. Even if you have a great document, some work may be needed in order to make that document admissible.

Years ago, I was called by a client contact from a large company that I had represented for some time. She had good news for me, she said, a big new lawsuit that was going to involve substantial effort. She even kidded me about how much money my law firm was going to make on the case, and told me she would send me the file of key documents by overnight mail. I called her back late the next day. No, my firm was not going to earn large fees on this case, and no, this was not going to be a big lawsuit. Why? Because we were going to settle this case before the plaintiff's lawyers saw our documents, that's why. Whatever their current demand was, we would pay it now. That's how bad a couple of those documents were. Sometimes it only takes one. We got the settlement, and the client probably saved millions.

The Ground Rules of Assessment:

- Your story may only be as good as your weakest storyteller.

- If a corporate defendant has to defend a bad act, or a bad actor, the jury may forgive the plaintiff almost anything.

- Your lawyer must understand the legal issues that apply to your dispute **before** you develop your strategic plan, or before you do discovery. An initial legal assessment, both of the substantive legal issues in the case and of the evidentiary issues that are anticipated, is indispensable to the initial assessment.

- Your lawyer must make sure to take a totally fresh approach to your case, and appreciate the dangers of routinizing his attitudes. This is a particular risk with lawyers who often handle the same kind of matter. If you sense that your lawyer believes that all corporations are evil, or all borrowers are deadbeats, or all injury claimants are malingerers, or all emotional distress claims are exaggerated, then tell your lawyer to throw that cookie cutter away. What happened in the last 50 cases doesn't matter. It is only this story and this evidence that matters.

- Pay attention to new developments, and to new information. Don't get stuck in your initial plan or your initial assessment if it turns out to be wrong, and or if things change.

- Beware the "sliding scale" of assessment. With some lawyers, every case is a great case when it comes in the door and a far more dangerous case 30 days before trial. Make sure that the initial assessment is realistic, and that any changes in the assessment can be explained properly by changes in the evidence or changes in other circumstances that bear upon the case.

- Make sure you get an initial assessment from your lawyer, and that you are communicating effectively with your lawyer in the process of developing that assessment, so that you and your lawyer are on the same page about what the assessment is, and what will cause a change in that assessment. Manage this process with the "why?" question.

II.

THE THREE PHASES OF A LAWSUIT

Once you have selected a lawyer, developed an initial assessment of your case, considered immediate settlement or mediation, and considered any other immediate steps you need to take in connection with the dispute, you enter the three principal phases of the lawsuit itself. Those phases are the strategic planning, the investigation and discovery, and the battle itself. Although we discuss these phases separately, they don't necessarily occur sequentially. In other words, you do not begin and complete the first phase, and then proceed to the second one. They overlap. For example, you develop a strategic plan at the outset of the case, but that planning process is ongoing thereafter, throughout the investigation, discovery, and even trial.

As we have discussed, people tend to think of a lawsuit as something that is won or lost at trial. That is how it is usually portrayed in the movies, and in the press. And, that is true in some cases. However, I think that **most** cases are won or lost in the strategic planning and in the depositions. The strategic planning is the chess game in the lawsuit, and, more than anything else, it separates the good lawyers from the bad lawyers. The really bad lawyers do little or no strategic planning at all. Inexperienced lawyers don't know how to do strategic planning properly.

Depositions are part of the discovery phase, when the testimony of witnesses and the parties is taken under oath, before trial. This is where the story gets locked in. This is where the witnesses disclose their testimony, get painted into corners, and expose their weaknesses. This is where your **themes** and **theory of the case** are either developed or disintegrate. Each phase of the lawsuit is critical, and understanding the role of each is important both for the client and for the lawyer.

Chapter 9

The Strategic Plan

The strategic plan for your lawsuit flows from the results of the Initial Assessment. You have developed a clear initial impression of what the case is all about, and you have initially "graded" the case, the witnesses, and the other evidentiary materials. You have a good initial handle on what the legal issues in the case are. Now, you are ready to plan. No general would go into battle without a war plan. You shouldn't either. A general understands that there is more to winning the war than getting the army to the battlefront, or even training the troops, or even developing a great battle plan to defeat the other side. It is also the little things, the details, that can make or break the campaign. If you send an army halfway around the world to battle, and don't have a plan for how to get them food, they will run out of food. If winter comes, and if they have the wrong clothing or equipment, their other strategic advantages may become useless.

You may remember the old proverb "For want of a nail the shoe was lost, for want of a shoe the horse was lost, for want of a horse the message was lost, for want of a message the battle was lost, for loss of the battle a kingdom was lost...." The basic purpose of a strategic plan is to make sure that all of the nails are where they belong.

The Ground Rules for a Strategic Plan

- Have a reason for everything that you do.
- Have a reason for **what**, have a reason for **when**, and have a reason for **how** you do it.
- Make sure that there is not a routine approach to your case, but that it is tailored to a thoughtful, fresh, and creative analysis of this particular dispute.
- Base your plan on a comprehensive understanding of the legal issues that will surface in the lawsuit.
- Begin immediately to develop your **themes** and your **theory of the case**.
- Plan for what discovery you need to get from others, and what you can do to minimize or control the discovery of adverse evidence from your side.
- Think about your case from the vantage point of your opponent's lawyer. How would you try to undermine your own lawsuit if you were on the other side? Consider carefully the rapport that both you and your lawyer have with opposing counsel and the opposing party. Do everything possible to maintain your **credibility** with them. Credibility with the opposition is a weapon that is often overlooked.
- Address your document control and witness management issues aggressively, and continuously.
- Pay attention to new developments and facts; don't get stuck in the initial plan or the initial assessment if it is wrong. Reassess and re-strategize frequently.

Planning the Tone

Having a reason for everything that you do sounds like a simple concept. It is not. In normal life, we do many things as a result of habit, style, imitation, our personality—or simply reactively. Although litigation certainly is not normal life, many lawyers approach it in the same way. A great example is with what I call the "tone of the case." A surprising number of lawyers have only one note in their horn. If it is their style to be aggressive or hostile, well, that's how they approach every case, and every adversary. They will treat the grieving widow just like they do the lying corporate executive.

A word about style—there is no best style for a lawyer. As I point out carefully to beginning litigation associates, there are hundreds of styles out there, and great lawyers who are equally effective being animated or calm, bombastic or reserved, dramatic or understated, passionate or analytical. The key, first, if you are the lawyer is to be yourself, and not to try to be what you are not. There are some great trial lawyers who sound like preachers delivering a sermon when they argue to the jury. If I tried to imitate that style, I would simply make a fool of myself—it is not me.

Whatever a lawyer's basic style may be, however, there is no excuse for approaching every case or witness the same way. They are different. At the beginning of the case, you and your lawyer can impact, even perhaps dictate, the tone of the case. That tone may have critical strategic importance, and so planning it is important too.

Based upon your initial assessment, what are the goals

here? Is there a reason to be hostile, or conciliatory? Is the opponent someone you have truly offended, angered, or hurt? Are they crooks trying to see how far they can push you and how much they can intimidate you? Are they basically reasonable people with whom you have a disagreement, people you may be able to persuade to see your side or at least to meet you halfway, if you treat them with respect? Is the goal to settle or fight all the way? Think carefully about why you are approaching opposing counsel and their client the way that you are.

The issue of credibility with your opponent is also one that is often overlooked, and underestimated in terms of its importance. Most lawyers understand the importance of maintaining credibility with the court, but many don't appreciate the value of maintaining credibility with the opposition. In the name of being "aggressive," some lawyers will initiate their contacts with the opposition with arrogant commentary, bold predictions about quick victory, and derisions of the other side's case. However, when the case doesn't play out, in the ensuing weeks and months, as they have arrogantly predicted, they have established nothing more than their willingness to say anything and everything. What they have lost is a valuable weapon. The lawyer who does not make bold predictions that fail to come true, who does not pretend to know things he doesn't know, and who expresses predictions and opinions that play out accurately over time maintains credibility. How is that credibility a weapon? Here is one example: When his opponent sits down with him a year and a half later to negotiate a settlement, his credibility will inevitably have an intimidating impact on the negotiations. When he says

"I really don't believe that you're going to be able to prove your second claim," a little voice in his opponent's head will be saying "this guy has been right on the money with everything he's said so far for the last year and a half." When your goal is to win, you can't throw away any of your tools, and credibility is an important one.

Speaking of goals, always have a "Plan B." When your goal is to settle, always be prepared to try the case if you must. On the flip side, no matter how determined you are to try the case and kill the enemy, no matter how bitter the dispute becomes, a good lawyer always wants the back-door open just a crack, at least. Surprisingly often, in just this type of case, the parties suddenly realize that they would be smart to talk to each other and resolve the matter. Not infrequently, this results from their very style of litigation, and the bitterness of the dispute, which has caused them economic exhaustion. Some civil line of communication is always useful; sometimes it absolutely requires a neutral mediator. Every good war strategy has an exit strategy.

Planning the Legal Side of the Case

This is another one that seems so painfully obvious, and is so often honored in the breach. The legal side of the case includes what the law says about issues that exist in your lawsuit, what it says in terms of the rules of evidence that may apply to the key evidence that the parties may want to introduce, and it also includes what pretrial motions and strategies may be available to "win" part or all of your case before trial.

Unfortunately, many lawyers only think about legal issues superficially at the beginning of the case, figuring that they will get all of the boring research done when a motion has to be filed, or before trial. Ironically, many of the great courtroom lawyers are the biggest offenders here. Research is dull and it's more fun beating up witnesses and preparing a trial strategy. They assume that they know the basic law because they have seen other cases like this before. The problem with this approach is that, in the law, the devil truly is in the details. Generally understanding contract law, or securities law, or products liability, or whatever the subject may be, is simply not enough.

To understand the importance of this, you need to look at the litigation process backwards, starting at the end. At the end of the trial, the judge will tell the jury, very specifically, what the law is that they need to know to decide the case. Before this, the lawyers on both sides will have argued to the judge what, exactly, those instructions to the jury should say, pointing the judge to many specific prior published decisions in the books, with facts which are close to the facts of your case. The jury will then be given instructions like "if you find that Mr. Smith acted with conscious disregard for the safety of others, then you must find..." and, "conscious disregard can include such behavior as...." In other words, the judge in these instructions gives the jury the **formula** for deciding, on the evidence, what to do. Similarly, if the case is decided by the judge before trial by, for example, a motion for summary judgment, it is that same legal formula that the judge will use to throw, or not throw, the case out of court. Such a motion, like trial, will usually occur <u>after</u> most or all of the discovery is done.

So, you can see that it would be quite handy to know the legal formula <u>before</u> the pretrial testimony of Mr. Smith is taken. Thus, the importance of planning the legal side of the case. That planning is critical to evaluating the strength of your case, telling you what motions you should file and what motions may be filed against you—and it gives you two critical lists: a list of what witnesses might say and what documents might say that would <u>help</u> build your case, and the list of what might hurt.

If part of the trial is about Mr. Smith's behavior, and if recent appellate decisions suggest that if Mr. Smith did not take certain specific steps, his behavior is less defensible, opposing counsel will press to establish that he in fact did not take those steps. But if your lawyer doesn't read the cases until after the depositions are over—uh, oh!, he never asked! Your lawyer may lose a pretrial motion that he should have won, or go to trial without knowing what the answer will be before the jury hears it too. On the other side, if Smith's lawyer didn't read the cases, he won't have prepared Smith for those questions before the deposition, and if opposing counsel is prepared, Smith may give bad answers without appreciating their consequences.

Another possibility is that the cases say that if Smith did four things, the lawsuit against him should be thrown out of court. If Smith's lawyer knows this, he will try to get the other side to admit that Smith did those four things, setting up a motion to win the day.

The bottom line is that planning the legal side of the case gives you the road map for your discovery strategy.

Planning the Evidence Side of the Case

"Winning" requires making the most of the evidence, which means having a plan for documents, witnesses, and experts, all of which leads (based upon the legal formulae uncovered by your legal plan) to a discovery strategy.

Document Control

Both paper and electronic documents need to be (1) identified; (2) obtained; and (3) organized. The process of identifying documents means reviewing what documents you have in your possession and have located, making a list of the types of documents that you may well have somewhere, but have not yet found, and making a list of the kinds of documents that your opponent has that you need, or that other "third parties" (people not involved directly in the lawsuit) may have that you need as well. Your legal plan will give you important directions as to what kinds of documents you are looking for, and what documents may be important.

Next, you have to develop a plan for obtaining the documents that you don't have, either from the other side, or from third parties, and also develop a plan for obtaining your own records, which if you are an individual may be as simple as searching your garage, and if you are a large company will be a far more complicated adventure.

Finally, the documents in the case must be organized. This can be a very simple or a very complicated task, depending upon how many documents there are, and what kinds of documents they are. Good organization is critical, whether it is simply a function of making files, or whether it is having professionals generate a computer database that allows you to quickly find, sort, and search large numbers of records. In addition, please remember that it is not sufficient to have all of your documents in place and organized. Your team must also know the contents of those documents. The extent to which knowing the contents of all of the documents involves you personally, your lawyer, or members of that lawyer's team, will depend on the case.

Witness Control

You must develop a plan for controlling "your" witnesses, as well as those witnesses whom you hope to persuade to become "your" witnesses. You must identify who these people are, find out what they would have to say, and then develop a strategy for turning them into willing, helpful, and effective witnesses.

Once you determine who "your" witnesses are, you must decide how to handle each witness, and who will have a primary role in interacting with that witness. With difficult witnesses, careful consideration of this subject can have an important impact on the outcome of the case. With any witness, the rapport, both personal and professional, that your lawyer develops with those individuals will play a significant role in that witness' performance.

What kind of witness is this? He may be a happy and loyal colleague, or a not-so-happy but somewhat loyal employee, or an unhappy former employee. He may be calm and collected, or terrified at the prospect of testifying. He may be a very likeable and trustworthy person, or he may be the sort of individual that puts people off. He may be very bright, or not. He may be a highly educated senior manager, or an unsophisticated blue collar worker.

The first thing to remember about witnesses is that they are <u>people</u>. You won't forget that, but your lawyer may. As lawyers, we are used to the fray of litigation and we tend to focus narrowly on our goals in the case when we are working with witnesses. Lawyers can sometimes be insensitive, or even oblivious, to how this individual is processing the experience of being a witness. It is important to be sensitive to the fact that this process can produce substantial anxiety in some people. This can be true even with rather unimportant witnesses. Cases can involve serious accusations of wrongdoing against individual employees, often quite unfairly. Some people are seriously traumatized by the process. Remember that when this person decided to become your friend, your employee, or whatever their role may be in this drama, they did not necessarily sign up for battle. They may not be experiencing this process as just another routine part of their job, or of their relationship with you. The most important thing that you can do is make sure that they are <u>thoroughly prepared</u> for the process, in a fashion tailored to their individual personality and needs. Your lawyer needs to really get to know these people as people, and to tune in to what they will need in order to get them where you want them to go.

In a case that I once handled for a large company, there were two key witnesses whom the other side identified, and wanted to depose. I had to prepare these two individuals for the process of being grilled by the opposing counsel on the facts, and they were the two key players involved in those facts. The two witnesses were a senior manager, and a lower level employee. As I prepared these witnesses, the senior manager was rock solid, forceful, articulate, and teeming with self-confidence. The other employee was a nervous wreck, terrified at the prospect of testifying, and unsure of how to say what she had to say. Long story short, the employee testified first, showed up for her deposition, and did a great job. I succeeded in calming her down, and although she was a little nervous, she walked away comfortable with the process, and relieved that it was over. The next day was the deposition of the manager. She showed up to the deposition over an hour late, deeply embarrassed. She confided in me that the reason she was late was because after she had begun driving to the deposition, she had to turn around and go back home to change clothes. She had been so nervous that she had thrown up all over herself. These are people.

Planning the Experts

There are three basic categories of outside experts that your lawyer may need to involve in your lawsuit: **consulting experts, testifying experts, and litigation support**. Experts are expensive, but can be critical to winning your case. A plan must be developed to determine what kinds of experts you will need, when you will need them, and who they should be. As with other parts of the planning process, there is a tendency for many lawyers to wait longer than they should before they begin to think through issues concerning experts. There are some cases where you can wait until you are heading to trial before you actually retain experts; this is often not the case, however, and the decision to wait should be made only after the issue has really been thought through carefully.

Consulting experts are people hired by your lawyer, because of their expertise in a particular area, to help the lawyer with the case. An accountant may be hired to help with a case that involves accounting issues, a doctor may be hired to help with a case involving medical issues, and scientists or technical specialists may be hired to help in other kinds of cases. There are many possible examples of consulting experts.

Sometimes, people feel that they need to hire a lawyer who is an expert in the kind of problem involved in their lawsuit. This is in some instances a good idea, but if you are involved in a lawsuit, you need most of all to hire a lawyer who is an expert in handling lawsuits. Just because your lawsuit involves, say, whether a shopping center had a sufficient security system to prevent attacks in its parking lot, doesn't mean necessarily that you need to find a lawyer who has a history of trying security-in-parking lot cases. However, your lawyer may well want to retain an expert in the field of security, to advise. That expert may have many good ideas about how to approach your case, what your **theory of the case** should be in terms of what was done right or wrong, what documents to ask from the other side, and what questions to ask of the witnesses. All of this in turn suggests that, in such a case, you may want to be thinking about the need for that expert at the very beginning of the lawsuit. It won't help very much if you hire the expert after the key depositions have been taken, only to find out that there was a whole series of questions that should have, but was not, asked.

If your lawyer is absolutely certain that the expert will not be converted into a **testifying expert**, then your lawyer can openly share all of your side's strategic thinking about the case with the expert. This can be very helpful in terms of brainstorming the case, and getting expert advice without risk. An expert retained by your lawyer who is not going to testify is, in most cases, under what is called the "work product doctrine," safe from being forced to testify by the other side as to what they were told. However, many consulting experts are later converted into testifying experts, and your lawyer must thus really think through, from the beginning, whether that is a possibility.

Testifying experts are experts who are retained to testify at trial, on your behalf. Because court rules do not require lawyers to identify to the other side who their testifying experts are until shortly before trial, most testifying experts are retained first as consulting experts, and then later designated to testify. However, any expert witness who is designated to testify must then disclose every document they have seen, and everything they have been told by anyone about the matter. For this reason, lawyers who hire an expert that they think may wind up testifying are very careful about what they say to that expert, and what they show that expert. Eventually, everything said and shown to that expert will be disclosed to the other side before trial.

Testifying experts are used as expert witnesses, to

explain to the judge and to the jury things that most people do not understand, and to express opinions. In most instances, witnesses are not allowed to express an opinion in their testimony, unless they are designated as an expert. This is why most cases do involve expert witnesses. Any case involving technical issues, medical issues, accounting issues, calculations of losses or damages, science, technology, or any other specialized field of knowledge requires expert witnesses. At the beginning of the case, you should be discussing with your lawyer what types of expert witness may be needed to testify in your case if it goes to trial. You may want to retain them immediately to begin consulting with you. You also need to plan for the cost of hiring these people. Further, you have to think about what experts the other side is going to hire. In some cases, it is important to get the very best and most credible experts in a field, and in some cases there are only a few really good experts in that field in your geographic area. If you don't identify and hire the best person early in your case, you may find that your opposition has hired that person instead.

There are two <u>critical</u> factors in retaining a testifying expert: (1) will the jury, based upon this person's background and experience, believe that he is a real and credible expert; and (2) is this person a <u>good witness</u>, who is likable, believable, and can explain his material in a way that is interesting and easy to understand.

Litigation support experts are the people hired by your lawyer to help with the technical side of telling your story, or organizing your case. They can provide services such as data control and computer imaging, organizing large numbers of documents in data banks or imaging records or videotaped deposition testimony for graphic presentation at trial. They can also be graphic artists, working with your lawyer to develop provocative and effective visualizations of your story, with charts, diagrams, blow-ups, computer animations or other graphic techniques that will become part of making a powerful and interesting presentation to the jury and helping the jury to understand and visualize the points you are making in telling your story. In the modern trial, the importance of this part of the process cannot be over-emphasized, as we will discuss later.

Developing a Discovery Strategy

"Discovery" is the process of where, before trial, the two sides in a lawsuit find out what information the other side has, ask each other for information and for documents, and take the testimony of witnesses in order to find out what their trial testimony will be. In the next chapter, we will explore the reasons for this process, and how it works. Most discovery is in one of the following forms: **depositions**, where the testimony of a party to the lawsuit or a witness is taken, under oath, before the case goes to trial; **interrogatories**, where one side can ask the other to answer written questions, by providing written answers under oath; **requests for admissions**, where you can ask the other side to admit or deny the truth of certain statements or assertions, or of the authenticity of documents, again under oath; and **requests for production of documents**, where you can ask the other side to provide you all documents in their possession or under their control that are relevant to the case. Discovery can also involve obtaining the prior testimony of expert witnesses who have been designated as testifying experts, or requiring in some cases that individuals undergo medical examinations, or property inspections.

It is critical to develop a strategy and a plan for your discovery. Go back to the first two **ground rules** of your strategic plan: have a reason for everything that you do, and have a reason for when and how you do it. This basic principle is perhaps more important in the discovery phase of the lawsuit than in any other. Your lawyer cannot approach your case with a cookie cutter, doing things in this case the same way as he does them in all the other cases. What you do matters, but so does the order and timing of what you do, and how you do it.

In developing your discovery strategy, focus on the key goals that you have in this process. They are:

1. To find out what you need to know, and what you don't already know.

2. To get evidence that you need for trial, in the form that you need it, and to establish what you need to establish in order to get that evidence in a form that will be admissible at trial.

3. To lock the other side and their witnesses into helpful positions, and into corners that they cannot later get out of.

4. To get the evidentiary pieces of the puzzle to fit

into the legal formulae that the jury will be given in the form of the judge's instructions to the jury on the law, so that when the pieces come together with those formulae, you win.

5. To undermine the credibility of witnesses who will be testifying against you.

6. To manage, to the extent possible, the development of evidence that will harm your side of the case.

7. To keep, to the extent that you can, your thinking to yourself, and to control the disclosure of your strategic thinking as you respond to discovery sent by the other side.

8. To develop the **themes** and **theory of the case**. You are honing the plot of your story. You are setting the stage for your storytelling. You are tying into the story your visualizations, your images, your key phrases. If you have planned these elements from the beginning, and if your lawyer is careful and disciplined, then the trial will be transformed. The jury will hear and experience these **themes**, this **theory**, these images, these key phrases, and these visualizations, not only from the arguments made by your lawyer at the beginning and at the end of the trial, but they will all flow from the testimony of all of the witnesses, both friendly and unfriendly, and from all of the other evidence that it is presented to the jury at the time of trial.

Planning the Cost

Every activity costs money. It costs money not only in the form of your lawyer's time, but there are many out-of-pocket expenses as well. Given your current assessment of this lawsuit and your strategic plan, what is a reasonable budget? What can you afford? What is at stake? There may be many options in terms of activity, discovery, hiring of experts, and engaging your opponent; on the other hand, if you and your lawyer plan carefully the cost of the lawsuit, you may conclude that it simply is not possible, or does not make sense, to do everything that could be done. As with everything else in life, sometimes you have to make hard decisions about living within a budget, and about doing what you can afford to do, or what is reasonable to do under the circumstances.

It is quite common for a new client to tell his lawyer that he wants the lawyer to be "very aggressive." Clients are often angry when they enter a lawsuit, and they often believe that, in order to win, they must bully the other side, or at least not be bullied themselves. They want to unload their wrath and aggression on the enemy, believing that this aggression will increase their chances of winning, that it will intimidate the other side, or at least that it will be cathartic.

Not surprisingly, it is often this very type of client who is the first to complain passionately after receiving the first few monthly bills from her lawyer. If you tell your lawyer that you want him to be "very aggressive," the first thing that your lawyer should tell you is that "very aggressive" means "very expensive." Activity is money. The more aggressive your approach, the more activity you are generating, and the quicker your legal bills build up. If you want an aggressive approach, plan for the cost of that approach. Similarly, if you expect that the other side is going to be very aggressive, you need to plan for that as well. They may be in a position to increase the cost of the lawsuit, well beyond what is reasonably necessary, and unfortunately there may be little that you and your lawyer can do to stop that from happening. This is one of the unfortunate parts of the legal process. In many types of cases, one side of the lawsuit is in a position to cause the other side to expend far more than is reasonably necessary, simply by generating activity. It is a flaw in the system that no one has figured out a solution to.

Managing the Strategic Plan

- Make sure there is one.
- Manage with the "why" question.
- Make sure you understand what the plan is, and that you agree with it. This is the time to get "on the same page" with your lawyer as to how this case is going to be handled, as to strategy, and as to cost. The best strategic plans are usually the result of careful teamwork between the lawyer and the client.

Chapter 10

Investigation and Discovery

This phase has two distinct aspects. **Investigation** is your process of individual and internal fact-finding, outside of the legal process. You are the only one who decides what you are going to investigate, and how you're going to investigate it, and the results of your investigation are for your own use, not necessarily to be shared with the other side. The investigation may be conducted in part by you, or people working with you, and in part by your lawyer or people working with him. You may also use professional investigators or private detectives, and a good deal of investigation can be done on the Internet. There are many ways of finding things out, to help with your side of the case.

One of my cases involved a woman claiming huge losses from missing oil paintings. In support of her claim, she had photographs of the paintings, along with a very old appraisal of those paintings by one of the premier international art appraisal companies. The appraisal document was a copy, but appeared to be authentic. The appraisal company told us that there was no way to firmly verify the record, because the individual appraiser had long since left the company, and they had no other records. Based upon our instincts, and other information we had about this woman, we were very suspicious of this appraisal. After some significant effort, our private investigator was able to locate the actual gentleman who had performed the appraisal in question. Remarkably, he actually remembered these paintings. Yes, that was his appraisal. Yes, that was his signature on the appraisal. No, those were not the numbers that he had assigned as value for the paintings; the document had been altered. He remembered quite clearly that the paintings were junk! He made a great trial witness.

Discovery is a formal legal process for the exchange of information, under oath. It is important to understand the two key reasons why our legal system has created the discovery process: to avoid surprises, and to help people settle their cases. In the old movies and television programs, all cases went to trial. At trial, the case would usually take a dramatic turn with one or a few unexpected and shocking surprises. In almost every *Perry Mason* episode, the trial would end with some dramatic revelation of critical facts, unknown or undisclosed until that very moment, taking away the breath of all present, and proving the innocence of the poor defendant who was on the verge of being convicted.

Trial by ambush makes for good reading and good watching, but our legal system has concluded that it does not make for a good system of justice. A trial is not supposed to be about who has the best lawyer, or who can throw the best curveball. A trial is supposed to be about finding the truth, and about a just and fair result. That is why the law requires, in most cases, that both sides show their cards, and have an opportunity to question under oath all of the witnesses, before the case goes to trial. Interestingly, little of this process applies in criminal cases, but that is not our subject here. In any event, the legal system assumes that both sides will get a better and fairer trial if this discovery process has taken place first. It also believes that by having all of this information disclosed prior to trial, the trial will be more orderly, and the information will be presented better to the jury.

The second reason why the legal system requires this discovery process to take place is because, well, most cases don't go to trial at all. The great majority of cases settle, and the legal system, which is overwhelmed with lawsuits, desperately wants as many cases to settle as possible. One of the key aspects of discovery is that, for the most part, each side has to show its cards to the other. Obviously, this makes it easier to settle the case. If the lawyers on both sides have a very good idea of what the arguments and evidence are on the other side, it takes a lot of the guesswork out of predicting how the trial is likely to go, and what the odds are of winning or losing the case. In a poker game where no one shows any card, and thus no one knows what anyone else's cards are, the game is likely to last longer, often with at least one player having made a big mistake. But in a game where each player is showing some or most of their cards, most hands will end more quickly, and more players will fold more quickly. When you have all the facts concerning your cards, and the other side's cards, it does help make those kinds of decisions.

Sending Out Written Discovery

This is your chance to demand that the other side give you documents, and that they answer questions under oath that you can later use against them at trial. The first type of written discovery is called a Request for Admission. The other side must respond to these requests with either an admission, a denial, or an objection.

For example, suppose that you represent the employee, Mr. Smith, in a lawsuit against his former employer, Bad Co. You are suing for wrongful termination because Mr. Smith was fired, and he believes that Bad Co. fired him for blowing the whistle on illegal activities. A few of the Requests for Admissions that Smith would serve upon Bad Co. might read something like this:

Request for Admission No. 1:

Admit that Mr. Smith and Bad Co. never entered into any written contract for employment.

Request for Admission No. 2:

Admit that Mr. Smith was qualified to serve as the controller of Bad Co.

Request for Admission No. 3:

Admit that Bad Co. was legally obligated to disclose accurately all expenditures concerning projects for federal agencies.

Request for Admission No. 4:

Admit that Bad Co. failed to disclose accurately all expenditures for project "Mousetrap."

Request for Admission No. 5:

Admit that Mr. Smith had a reasonable and good faith belief that Bad Co. was not complying with its obligations to disclose all expenditures accurately on projects for federal agencies.

Request for Admission No. 6:

Admit that Mr. Smith complained to his superiors concerning failure by Bad Co. to properly disclose its expenditures.

The next form of written discovery is Interrogatories. These are questions that must be responded to.

In our same hypothetical case, Mr. Smith might send Bad Co. Interrogatories which include questions such as the following:

Interrogatory No. 1:

Please identify by name and last known address and telephone number all individuals who are responsible for the decision to terminate Mr. Smith.

Interrogatory No. 2:

Please state all reasons for the decision to terminate Mr. Smith.

Interrogatory No. 3:

If you contend that Mr. Smith was not qualified to perform the job of controller at Bad Co., please state all facts which support that contention.

Interrogatory No. 4:

If you contend that Bad Co. has obtained any information, since Mr. Smith's last day of work, which would support or justify his termination of employment, describe all such information, including but not limited to the source of that information

Interrogatory No. 5:

If you contend that Mr. Smith violated any statute, law, or regulation during his employment with Bad Co., state all facts which support that contention.

With Requests for Production of Documents, you can request that the other side produce to you all documents, notes, messages, emails, letters, and any other written record that they may have which is relevant to the lawsuit. The other side must identify and produce all such records, or file an objection to the request.

Demand for Production No. 1:

The complete contents of any personnel and/or employment file maintained by Bad Co. concerning Mr. Smith.

Demand for Production No. 2:

Any and all documents which constitute, evidence, reflect, refer, relate to, and pertain to the qualifications and experience required by Bad Co. for the position of controller.

Demand for Production No. 3:

All documents which you believe support your contention that Mr. Smith did not possess the qualifications and experience necessary to carry out the job responsibilities of controller.

Demand for Production No. 4:

If you contend that at any point in time the work of Mr. Smith was in any way deficient, each and every document which supports that contention.

Demand for Production No. 5:

Any and all documents which reflect, refer to, relate to, or pertain to Mr. Smith's job performance.

Demand for Production No. 6:

Any and all documents signed, written, or

authored by any of your agents or employees which in any way refer to Mr. Smith.

Demand for Production No. 7:

Any and all documents which reflect, refer to, evidence, or relate to any action taken by Bad Co. or on behalf of Bad Co. following any investigation into any complaint made by Mr. Smith.

Demand for Production No. 8:

Any and all documents which constitute, evidence, reflect, refer to, or relate to any counseling, warning, reprimand, or criticism, whether written or verbal, given to Mr. Smith for any reason at any time while Mr. Smith was employed by Bad Co.

Demand for Production No. 9:

Any and all documents which constitute, evidence, reflect, refer to, or pertain to any communication between Bad Co. and Mr. Smith concerning whether or not Bad Co. was accurately disclosing its expenditures.

Demand for Production No. 10:

Any and all tape recordings of any communications between anyone and Mr. Smith.

Demand for Production No. 11:

Any and all photographs, videotapes, or films depicting Mr. Smith.

There are several keys to sending out good written discovery to the other side. First, based upon your own investigation and research, you must be asking the right questions, and <u>all</u> of the right questions. Next, you want to be asking questions that are carefully written, approaching subjects both narrowly and broadly, so that you get everything that you need, and so that the other side is totally boxed into its responses. So, for example, you may ask them to produce "all demands that you claim to have sent for payment under the contract," along with "all documents that in any way refer to or concern the contract." At times, your requests are designed to obtain very specific things, or to establish that the other side has or does not have those things. At other times, you are casting a wide net, without necessarily knowing what you're going to get, but finding out what there is.

You do not want to go to trial and have the other side produce a document that you've never seen, and have them claim that they did not produce it because you never asked for it. Similarly, you do not want to be surprised by any witnesses or any facts, not disclosed by the other side, where they can legitimately claim that you never required them to produce that information. If you can point to written discovery sent by you where the information was requested, and establish that it was not produced or identified, the court may take one of a number of steps to punish the other side for that failure to disclose, including prohibiting them from using that information at trial, or letting you tell the jury that they were hiding information.

Remember to have a reason for everything you do, as well as for when and how you do it. Timing in discovery is important. For example, suppose that you are the defendant in a significant lawsuit. The complaint was recently filed, and the plaintiff has not taken any steps since then. You are in the process of investigating the facts on your side, and trying to find all of your records, but it will take you a while to complete that process, and you are at this point not quite sure of all of the facts or of what your position will be. Is this a good time to immediately send a long and comprehensive document request to the plaintiff? It may very well not be. Every action causes an equal and opposition reaction. The plaintiff's lawyers may be sleeping, or just waiting for something to happen; if you send them a long document request, you can bet your bottom dollar you're going to get one right back. And you may not be ready yet to respond to theirs! Further, the order in which you conduct discovery is very important. When you take the deposition of the defendant, he has to speak for himself. When you send him written interrogatories, his lawyer is going to draft those responses, with his help. Sometimes you want to ask a lot of technical questions in writing before you take a deposition, because you need this information in order to be prepared to take the deposition properly. Other times, you don't want to give an opportunity for the lawyer and the defendant to spend many hours working on carefully crafting their spin on every hard question while they work on answers to your interrogatories; you have simply provided the defendant with an organized speech to give you when you take his deposition. Responding to written discovery forces the lawyer and his client to work carefully together, and gets them organized and prepared in a way that they may otherwise not be. Early depositions can be very effective. They can also be a mistake. This is where the judgment of the lawyer becomes critical. The biggest dangers of taking an early deposition are that, after the deposition is completed, you will obtain documents or information from other sources that would have been important to examine the witness about, but now the opportunity is lost. Usually, you only get one crack at a witness. The key goals in written discovery are:

1. To find out what you need to know, and what you don't already know.

2. To get evidence that you need for trial, in the form that you need it, and to establish what you need to establish in order to get that evidence in a form that will be admissible at trial.

3. To lock the other side and their witnesses into helpful positions, and into corners that they cannot later get out of.

4. To get the evidentiary pieces of the puzzle to fit into the legal formulae that the jury will be given in the form of the judge's instructions to the jury on the law, so that when the pieces come together with those formulae, you win.

5. To undermine the credibility of witnesses who will be testifying against you.

6. To develop the **themes** and **theory of the case**. You are honing the plot of your story. You are setting the stage for your storytelling. You are tying

into the story your visualizations, your images, your key phrases. If you have asked your questions carefully and present the answers you receive at trial, the jury will hear and experience these **themes**, this **theory**, these images, these key phrases, and these visualizations, not only from the arguments made by your lawyer at the beginning and at the end of the trial, but from those answers as well.

Responding to Written Discovery

When you are responding to written discovery, the first and last rule is to always tell the truth and the whole truth. Your responses are under oath, and this is your absolute obligation. Of equal importance, failing to tell the truth and the whole truth is usually a major tactical blunder. In almost any lawsuit, each party has certain facts that are not particularly helpful; they may even be downright embarrassing. Each side has some documents that they wish did not exist. Understand that this is normal, and that it does not necessarily mean that you won't get what you want in the lawsuit. Also understand that, when people play games with the facts or with the documents, it rarely works. Trust me on this one. The overwhelming majority of the time, the bad facts come out. And this leads us to the issue of the monumental tactical error that you may commit by playing those games: As so many politicians and so many litigants have learned, you can cause yourself much more harm by trying to hide bad facts, than by admitting them. As we will discuss shortly, my first goal with any opposing party, no matter what the case is, is to attack his credibility if he gives me an opportunity to do so. I don't care what the case is about; if I can catch you lying, or trying to hide something, or trying to gloss over something important, I will make you pay, and pay, and pay. If you are on the other side, you do <u>not</u> want to give me that opportunity.

All of this having been said, a good lawyer knows when objections can properly be made to written discovery, and knows how to craft answers so that he answers, narrowly, the question that has been asked. Bad questions will get less useful answers. There are, in fact, opportunities presented often by sloppy questioning on the part of the other side. There will be times where, while being completely truthful, you can avoid disclosing bad facts or bad documents to the other side if they are poorly skilled at drafting their requests. These are judgment calls which must be made very, very carefully. Some lawyers are very skilled at both writing and responding to written discovery, and this can really make a big difference in the outcome of some cases.

In responding to written discovery, your primary goals are:

1. To manage, to the extent possible, the development of evidence that will harm your side of the case.

2. To keep, to the extent that you can, your thinking

to yourself, and to control the disclosure of your strategic thinking as you respond to discovery sent by the other side.

3. To develop the **themes** and **theory of the case**. You are honing the plot of your story. You are setting the stage for your storytelling. You are tying into the story your visualizations, your images, your key phrases. If you answer discovery carefully, the jury will hear and experience these **themes**, this **theory**, these images, these key phrases, and these visualizations, not only from the arguments made by your lawyer at the beginning and at the end of the trial, but from those responses as well.

Pay particular attention to goal number three. In responding to written discovery, you are beginning to tell your side of the story. These responses may be read to the jury, or given to the jury. If you have developed your **themes**, your **theory**, and your images, you can begin to load these in all of your written responses to questions. This, in turn, will help to keep your story and your message consistent at trial.

Taking Depositions

A deposition is a proceeding where the testimony is taken, under oath and prior to trial, of a party or of a witness. Many cases are won or lost in the depositions. The deposition usually takes place in a conference room at the office of the attorney who is taking the deposition. All parties and their attorneys can attend the deposition and all lawyers can participate in it. When the lawyer who has requested the right to take the deposition has finished his questions, then the other lawyers can ask their questions. The lawyer representing the witness "defends" the deposition.

There is a certified court reporter attending the deposition, who swears in the witness before the testimony begins, with the same oath that the witness would take if testifying before a judge at trial. Testimony given at a deposition is under penalty of perjury. The court reporter transcribes everything that is said at the deposition, and then generates a transcript which is made available to the lawyers, and which the witness gets an opportunity to review after the deposition is finished. The witness can make any changes or additions to his testimony, or corrections to the transcript, but all changes can be brought to the attention of the judge and jury at the time of trial.

The lawyers who are not taking the deposition or who are defending the deposition have the right to object to any question asked, under strict rules of evidence. During the depositions, the lawyers will often push and test each other in the course of objecting to questions and arguing about the objections to questions. This is particularly true at the beginning of a case, as the lawyers try to measure each other up. If a lawyer believes that the other lawyer is behaving unreasonably, inappropriately, or not following the rules of procedure or evidence correctly, that lawyer can make a motion to the court, and the court will decide what to do about it. Motions can also be made if a witness refuses to answer a question, or where a lawyer objects to a question and instructs the witness not to answer the question.

Although the rules of procedure and evidence are designed to create clear and narrow guidelines for the behavior of lawyers in depositions, the proceedings often stray from those narrow guidelines. The fact is that it is quite common for experienced or skillful lawyers to push around and take advantage of less experienced and less skillful lawyers in depositions. The deposition process is where the real hand-to-hand combat between the lawyers begins in a lawsuit, and quite often it is where it ends as well, either by setting up the lawsuit for a motion that brings the case to a conclusion, or by forcing one of the parties to settle, or by locking in the witnesses in such a fashion that the outcome of the trial is largely determined before it begins.

Depositions are normally not intended to be the trial testimony of the witness; they are intended to be the testimony of the witness prior to that witness testifying live before the judge or jury at trial. However, sometimes, the deposition becomes the entire trial testimony of the witness; this can occur, for example, if the witness dies before trial, or is legally "unavailable" at the time of trial. For instance, a witness who lives in another state or another country may not be subject to being forced to come to the trial, and the deposition may become that witness' trial testimony.

However, even if the witness does testify at trial, portions of the deposition may be used by any of the lawyers in the case during the trial. This typically occurs when a lawyer believes that a witness has contradicted his testimony, and the jury is allowed to hear or see the deposition testimony, to determine whether or not the witness is changing his story. Because of the various uses that can be made of deposition testimony at trial, one key decision that must be made when your lawyer is taking a witness' testimony is to decide whether or not to videotape the deposition. Court rules permit the videotaping of a deposition, and if it is videotaped, you may be permitted to show portions of that testimony to the jury at trial. If there is no videotape of the deposition, the prior testimony of the witness must be read to the jury; this is obviously less effective in many respects. First, it is very boring to have something read to you, and people tend to pick up little of what is being read to them. Moreover, the reading of a transcript does not give you some of the most important aspects of the testimony. Seeing how long the witness paused after hearing the question before answering, watching the witness' face as she tries to think up her answer, seeing how nervous she is while she is answering— all of this provides, potentially, very important information to the jury that does not flow from reading a transcript.

Computer programs permit a lawyer to maneuver, instantly, to any portion of the prior testimony of a witness, while that witness is being cross-examined. Thus, at trial, after asking questions of the witness before the jury, the lawyer can immediately flash onto a screen the prior testimony of the witness on the same subject. This can be devastatingly effective as a form of cross-examination. However, as we have discussed before, all good things cost money. Videotaping a deposition increases the cost of that deposition substantially, as does the use of the technology required to show videotaped deposition segments to a jury at trial. Decisions have to be made, in each case, whether the cost is justified.

Taking a deposition is not simply about giving the witness the opportunity to tell you what that witness feels like telling you about the facts of the lawsuit. Good lawyers can have a dramatic impact upon what witnesses say, and how they come across. In this process of recording what the witnesses have to say about the case, the quality of the lawyering often makes a very big difference in the direction that the case takes. Without trying to identify all of the subtleties that come to play in the proper cross-examination of witnesses, seven key factors can be identified which separate the excellent lawyer taking a deposition from the rest:

First, there is **preparation**. It is appalling how often lawyers show up to take a deposition without having properly prepared, and it always shows. If your lawyer does not understand the legal issues, the facts, and the documents before taking the deposition, opportunities will be lost, sometimes with critical consequences. If your lawyer has not taken the time to really think about all of the areas of questioning that should be explored with this witness, again, opportunities will be lost. Preparation means knowing every aspect of the case that the witness may have information about, and every document that must be shown to the witness during the examination. It means understanding every issue where this witness may be willing, or pushed, to help you tell your side of the story, and also understanding every issue where this witness wants to, or is capable of, harming your side of the case. Bad lawyers hit the obvious points, and good lawyers go much, much further.

Next, it is critical before beginning a deposition to have a **strategy**. A strategy means knowing why you are taking this witness' deposition now, rather than earlier or later in the discovery process. It means understanding whether this is a witness that you want to push into being cautious and careful about his testimony, or whether you want this witness to become comfortable with the process and open up, volunteering her opinions, recollections, and impressions. Having a strategy means understanding what role this witness has, or may be manipulated into having, as a storyteller for key aspects of the story in this case. It also means understanding how this witness can help you develop your **themes** and **theory of the case**. Having a strategy means having an approach to impacting this witness' attitude about testifying and this witness' frame of mind while testifying. If the witness is adverse, it means having a strategy for how to impeach the credibility of the witness, to get the witness to contradict himself, or contradict other witnesses on his side of the case, or to contradict documents that you may introduce into evidence.

At the deposition itself, the single most important thing to be done by the lawyer taking the deposition is **listening**. That's right. The single most important thing to do when examining a witness is to listen. Although this sounds like a simple task, it is one of the most common weaknesses in litigators, a weakness that is being exacerbated by technology. When lawyers are asking questions, they usually have an outline of the issues they want to examine the witness about, and some idea of where they are going with the examination. Unfortunately, they often pay less attention to listening very carefully to what the witness is saying. The lawyer who knows how to listen picks up on the subtle and often unexpected signals that the witness gives about additional information they may have, or about unexpected areas of examination that ought to be explored.

Years ago, trial lawyers tended to develop better listening skills, because more cases went to trial, and because there were fewer visual crutches and distractions to keep them from listening. Today, fewer cases go to trial, and many lawyers spend most of their time, while sitting in front of a witness, staring at their computer screen or at documents. While these tools can be helpful when used effectively, they can also present a serious distraction to careful listening, resulting in poor examination of the witness. Listening skills do not develop automatically. We are all programmed to learn and absorb information far more easily with our eyes than with our ears, and technology only pushes us further in that direction. Great lawyers are great listeners. In a deposition, one of the most important benefits of listening carefully is knowing what kind of a record you have. Getting a great admission out of a witness in a deposition is not all that useful, if the testimony is garbled. The testimony can be garbled either because your question was lousy, or because the witness' answer was inarticulate. A good lawyer can hear whether her question was clear, and whether the answer was clear; if it wasn't, that lawyer will follow up and get it clear before moving on to another topic.

Next, the lawyer at a well-taken deposition is **locking in** the storyteller. This is not just about hearing what the witness has to say. It is painting the witness into a corner with her story so that she cannot, at trial, add or expand to it in ways that are damaging to you. The following example is real testimony, edited somewhat to protect the innocent:

Q. Do you have a recollection of seeing this performance evaluation before?

A. Yes.

Q. Did you sign this document?

A. Yes.

Q. Do you recall the events that are discussed in this document?

A. Yes.

Q. Are the criticisms made of you correct?

A. No.

Q. The first column of the performance appraisal discusses your performance on hiring and staffing, do you see that?

A. Yes.

Q. And the comment is "George trains his associates well, and has a good working relationship with his staff." Do you see that?

A. Yes.

Q. Did you agree with that comment when you saw it?

A. Yes.

Q. The next column discuses administration.

A. Yes, it does.

Q. It says "George processes his paperwork accurately and on a timely basis." Did you agree with that comment?

A. Yes.

Q. The next column discusses the issue of communication, and says "George communicates well with his staff." Do you see that?

A. Yes.

Q. Did you agree with that comment?

A. Yes.

Q. The performance evaluation goes on to say that you need to do a better job of listening to your supervisors. Did you agree with that comment?

A. No.

Q. The next item also contains a criticism of your performance. Did you agree with that criticism?

A. No.

Q. Would it be fair to say that you agree with everything positive stated in this evaluation, and that you disagree with everything negative stated in this evaluation?

A. Yes.

Several things were locked in for this witness' testimony at trial. First, at the time of his evaluation, he saw that evaluation, signed it, and understood the document. Second, he thought about and considered each and every item in that evaluation, and understood what it was that his supervisor was criticizing him about. Third, he disagreed with any form of criticism that he received, and thought his supervisor was right whenever he received praise, but thought his supervisor was wrong whenever he was criticized. (The actual questioning on the document was longer, as there was a long series of disagreements with the numerous criticisms contained in the evaluation.)

Remember that the witness will have plenty of time, before trial, to review her testimony and to think about how she could improve it. If you have left doors open for her to improve her story, you have missed an opportunity. There are numerous examination techniques that your lawyer can use to accomplish this result, but the story of any witness that has given a deposition must be locked in, to minimize the possibility of new and surprising revelations at the time of trial. Poor deposition examination often results in the lawyer thinking that they know what that witness will testify to, and then being confronted with unpleasant and unexpected testimony in front of the jury.

In addition, great cross-examination never loses sight of the critical issue with any witness: **credibility**. Your lawyer cannot change what a hostile witness or adverse party wants to testify to, testimony that may be very damaging to your story. However, a witness can hurt you much less if he has lost his credibility, and good lawyers know how to attack the credibility of a witness. This can be far more subtle and complex than just confronting them with an accusation that they are lying.

Q. Is this document a statement you prepared to respond to your performance evaluation?

A. Yes, it is.

Q. Is the first paragraph your response concerning your relationship with your supervisor?

A. Yes, it is.

Q. In this document, you state "Suzanne is a wonderful mentor and totally knowledgeable as to all facets of the company." Do you see that?

A. Yeah.

Q. Is it true that she was a wonderful mentor?

A. No.

Q. Why did you say that?

A. To try to retain my job.

Q. So you were willing to lie in this document in order to look good to your boss?

A. Yes.

In the above examination, first we have authenticated an important document, establishing that he prepared it and remembers it. Next, we established that he intentionally lied, by his own hand, in order to manipulate his boss. He writes warm and grandiose praise of a woman that he could not stand, simply to get what he wanted. Why wouldn't he lie to the jury, to get money? Juries understand that people who lie and manipulate in order to achieve their purposes cannot be trusted.

Good cross-examination can reveal that a witness'

memory is not reliable, or that a witness is selective in the detail they remember about the facts, clearly remembering certain things and conveniently forgetting others. Good cross-examination can reveal inconsistencies in the witness' story, or contradictions between that witness and other witnesses, or contradictions between the witness' testimony and documents. If a witness is not telling the truth, or trying too hard to "spin" the facts, or trying too hard to help one side of the case, good lawyering can bring these qualities of the witness to the harsh light of day, and minimize, perhaps even eliminate, the harm of that witness' testimony to your case. Moreover, when dealing with the credibility of a party, a successful attack on the credibility of that individual can, by itself, win the case. When a person who is bringing a lawsuit is caught inventing or exaggerating facts, this can be enough to end their chances of winning. When a defendant who is accused of wrongdoing is caught hiding information or contradicting his own records, his case may be lost. The lesson from this is that when you are in a lawsuit, never lose your credibility. If there is a bad fact, or a bad document, you are far better off conceding it, no matter how bad it is, than being painted effectively as a liar.

Another critical factor in the deposition of witnesses is the use of **documents**. There are several aspects of this. First, the deposition must reveal what the witness knows about key documents in the case, and what the witness can add to those documents (for example, by having a recollection of the meeting that is discussed in the letter). Effective cross-examination of a witness involves skillful use of exhibits at the deposition, knowing when and how to use those exhibits. For example, if there is a document that describes in detail what happened at a meeting that the witness attended, the skillful lawyer will often ask the witness to testify as to his best recollection of the meeting before showing him the document. The witness may not have seen the document recently, and may give a different version of what happened from what the document reveals. Contradicting the document will in turn provide an opportunity to impeach the credibility of the witness, or perhaps of the author of the document.

Q. And what did you do in 2003?

A. I went to work for Long's Drug Company.

Q. In what position?

A. First Assistant Store Manager.

Q. How long did you work for them?

A. About a year.

Q. Did your title change during that time?

A. No.

Q. What title did you have when you left Long's?

A. The same, First Assistant Store Manager.

Q. What was your next job after Long's?

A. I went to work for Bill's Auto Parts.

Q. And what position did you have at Bill's Auto Parts?

A. First Assistant Store Manager.

* * *

Q. When you were working as First Assistant Store Manager at Long's, what were your job functions?

A. Scooping ice cream, putting away stock, unloading trucks, cashiering, and other menial work.

Q. Did you have any management functions?

A. No.

Q. Was there any part of your job that you considered to be management work?

A. No.

Q. You didn't really think that anything you did was management?

A. No.

* * *

Q. Let me show you what's been marked as Exhibit 1 to your deposition. Is this the application you provided to our client when you applied for a position as a manager?

A. Yes.

Q. At the top, the first item that you have is your present employment with Bill's Auto Parts. Do you see that?

A. Yes.

Q. And it says that the position you hold is that of manager. Do you see that?

A. Yes.

Q. Isn't it true that in fact you were the First Assistant Manager?

A. To me it's the same.

Q. So you thought that Assistant Manager and Manager meant the same thing?

A. First Assistant Manager was almost being a manager. It was being the manager when the manager was gone, which was more than half the time. Hiring, firing, merchandising.

Q. Did you think that "almost a manager" meant the same thing as "manager?"

A. Yes.

Q. Were you trying to represent to our client that your position at Bill's Auto Parts was in fact being the top manager?

A. No.

Q. As opposed to the Assistant Manager?

A. No.

Q. What about with regard to Long's? Do you see the second item on your job application?

A. Yes.

Q. Again, you were an Assistant Manager at Long's, weren't you?

A. I was First Assistant Manager, meaning I was almost a manager.

Q. But you were the First Assistant Manager, weren't you? That was your title?

A. Yes.

Q. But you put down that you were a manager.

A. Yes.

Q. Why didn't you write down that you were a First Assistant Manager?

A. Just to look better.

First, we have set up the use of this gentleman's employment application by asking him some questions about his prior jobs. He has carefully remembered the titles that he held, and remembers that none of these jobs involved any real management. He is stressing that point because he is thinking about his own theory in support of his lawsuit, which is that managers at big retail companies don't do any real managing, they just do menial work. This was an overtime wage claim. Next, he authenticates the employment application that he filled out in order to get the job with our client. He probably had not seen this document in quite a while, and did not remember what was in it. Now, he is forced to admit that he lied about the positions that he held in his prior jobs. When it comes to his job responsibilities, this witness will now have to choose between his lies, and as to which one he wants to admit. Either he lied about his prior job responsibilities in his job application, or he has been lying in his testimony when he says that he never really did any actual management work in any of these positions. Clearly, whatever he tells the jury about his work experience is a moving target that changes to suit the convenience of the moment.

Another important role of documents in the deposition is that, before trial, the lawyer must have the ability to prove the authenticity of any document that he wants to introduce at trial. Sometimes, just showing a document to a witness and having them establish that it is their signature, that they wrote it, or that they know what it is, may provide a critical step necessary for getting that document admitted into evidence at the time of trial.

Finally, skillfully taking a deposition means developing your **themes** and **theory of the case**. While taking a deposition, the lawyer does this not only by selecting the questions to be asked, but also by carefully selecting the words used to ask the question.

Q. You were criticized for things you said to employees in the workplace, weren't you?

A. Yes.

Q. Were those criticisms fair?

A. No.

Q. Do you know who Lucy Ross, R-O-S-S, is?

A. Yes.

Q. Please look at Exhibit No. 2, which is a statement written by her. Have you ever seen this document before?

A. I know about this incident.

Q. What do you know about it?

A. I personally knew that I had made a slip. I used to say "bite" me all the time. And somehow—I don't know how—the word "blow" me came out. I apologized to her. I told her I was sorry. Because I always used to say to my wife "bite me" because there was something on the radio or TV or some movie that I had watched that said "bite me." It just meant "leave me alone."

Q. Well, did you think that "bite me" was substantially more polite than "blow me?"

A. Yes.

Q. Why is that?

A. It just is.

Q. Did you think that "bite me" was an appropriate thing for a manager to say to someone who reports to that manager in the workplace?

A. We all talk like that to each other. And I don't believe the store was open.

Q. Putting aside whether there were customers present, as you sit here today, based upon your experience as a manager, do you think it's appropriate in the workplace for a manager to say to a subordinate "bite me"?

A. It was a way to say "leave me alone," or "get out of my face."

* * *

Q. Did you ever have any arguments with your supervisor in front of customers?

A. No. We would have discussions. She would think that I should do something differently.

Q. What, in your mind, is the difference between an argument and a discussion?

A. One has two sides; and one has one side.

Q. Which one has only one side?

A. An argument. One person is yelling at the other person. A discussion, two people are talking or yelling back and forth or discussing back and forth.

We may have succeeded in establishing several things about this witness. First, that he is a creep. Second, that he has no judgment whatsoever. Third, that he does not appear to have a clue as to what constitutes appropriate behavior by a manager interacting with a subordinate, or with a superior. Fourth, that he will say absolutely anything to rationalize his behavior. Given that this case involves this gentleman's termination, the only question the jury may have for my client is, what took you so long? Sometimes, when it comes to the effort of trying to make a witness look bad, the witness is willing to do much of the heavy lifting.

If there are certain catchwords, phrases, or visualizations that the lawyer is going to want to use repeatedly while arguing to the jury at trial, that presentation will be made far more effective if those same phrases and words are used by the lawyer in questions at the depositions. The skillful lawyer will get the witness to agree with those characterizations, or even to begin using them himself in his answers. If the lawyer is going to want to establish, at trial, that a defendant was arrogant, or that a car was screeching around the corner, or that a child was small and vulnerable, or that an accident victim was in great pain, the careful selection of words or phrases during the examination of various witnesses in the case may lead to a pattern of language used in the testimony, and brought before the jury, which establishes the picture of the facts that he wants the jury to see.

In taking a deposition, the key goals of the lawyer are:

1. To find out what you need to know, and what you don't already know.

2. To get evidence that you need for trial, in the form that you need it, and to establish what you need to establish in order to get that evidence in a form that will be admissible at trial.

3. To lock the other side and their witnesses into helpful positions, and into corners that they cannot later get out of.

4. To get the evidentiary pieces of the puzzle to fit into the legal formulae that the jury will be given in the form of the judge's instructions to the jury on the law, so that when the pieces come together with those formulae, you win.

5. To undermine the credibility of witnesses who will be testifying against you.

6. To manage, to the extent possible, the development of evidence that will harm your side of the case.

7. To develop the **themes** and **theory of the case**. The jury will hear and experience these **themes**, this **theory**, these images, these key phrases, and these visualizations, not only from the arguments made by your lawyer at the beginning and at the end of the trial, but they will all flow from the testimony of all of the witnesses, both friendly and unfriendly, and from all of the other evidence that it is presented to the jury at the time of trial.

Defending Depositions

Your lawyer will defend you when your deposition is taken, and will defend (whether or not he acts officially as their counsel at the deposition) witnesses helpful to your side of the case. As with the taking of depositions, the two keys prior to defending a deposition are being prepared and having a strategy, and the most important thing to do for the lawyer defending a deposition is to be listening carefully to what is being said by both the lawyers and the witness.

When you are having your deposition taken, your lawyer should prepare you very thoroughly for the process. First, your lawyer must explain to you what to expect at the deposition and how the procedure works. You are going to be nervous at your deposition, but the more prepared you are for the procedure, the more comfortable you will be. You should be told where the deposition will take place, who will attend, how long it is likely to last, how you should dress for the deposition, and how you should behave at the deposition. Your lawyer should explain to you what will happen at the beginning of the deposition, including the types of personal questions about your background that will probably be asked, even though they may not appear to you to be relevant to the case. You need to be told what to do if you want a break, if you need to use the restroom, if you want to ask your lawyer a question, or if you are getting irritated. You need to be told what to do if you don't understand the question, or if you are not sure of what the answer to the question is, or if you don't remember something that you are being asked, or if you have some recollection but a poor recollection of the facts. You should be told how to deal with different types of questions, how to deal with a pushy lawyer, and what to do when your lawyer is objecting to questions. You should be told how to listen to questions, and how much you should be volunteering information beyond what the answer to the question is. If you have not been through the deposition process before, or even if you have, your lawyer may find it helpful to spend some time pretending to take your deposition, and giving you a "trial run" on how to listen to questions and then answer them correctly.

In preparing for your deposition, make sure to do your homework, and make sure that your lawyer helps you do your homework. Know the facts you need to know, and be familiar with the documents you should be familiar with.

Your lawyer may make judgment calls about what you need to study, and what you don't need to study. Ask all of the questions of your lawyer that you have about the process, and about your testimony. Listen very carefully to your lawyer's instructions, and trust them.

When you are testifying at your deposition, the first cardinal rule is to tell the truth and whole truth. Don't play games. As we have discussed before, if you are like most people in a lawsuit, there are going to be some facts that don't help you, that you wish were not there. However, telling the truth is not only something you will do because you have sworn to do so; it is something you are going to do because you are smart and you want to win. Playing games almost always backfires, and the downside of getting caught playing games is far worse than facing up to the truth and giving your lawyer a chance to help you win your case under the circumstances as they are. Also, carefully follow your lawyer's advice and instructions. This is not the time to be second-guessing whether you agree with your lawyer's approach to the case. Don't try to be a lawyer, and don't try to out-think your lawyer in preparing for and giving your deposition.

Most people are nervous before their deposition, and are concerned that being nervous will harm their testimony. Most witnesses discover that fear and nervousness is not their principal problem while testifying. Being a little nervous at the beginning is completely normal, and is expected by everyone, including a jury at trial. At a deposition, most witnesses find that the butterflies go away after a few minutes of answering questions, particularly the routine questions that typically are asked at the beginning of depositions. What you have to really fight at a deposition is not so much nerves as boredom and frustration. In the first half hour of your deposition, when you are anxious and alert, it is much easier to listen very carefully to the question (as your lawyer told you to do), to answer only the question that has been asked, and to not answer a question if you don't understand it. This is much harder to do hours later, when you are tired, and when the lawyer seems to be asking you the same question over and over. It is easy to get tired of the process, and frustrated with the process. That is when careful preparation and discipline make the difference, taking breaks when you need them, but taking every question one question at a time, listening to it carefully, and giving a thoughtful reply. As a witness, the deposition is about two things: What is the question? And, what is the answer?

If you are having your deposition taken in a lawsuit where you are a party, you may be tempted to spar with the lawyer on the other side. You may also find that the lawyer does what he can to draw you into that kind of a fight. Don't do it. Do not get into arguments with the other lawyer, and do not try to figure out what the other lawyer is doing and why. These are very common mistakes, and they are almost always big mistakes. First, arguing with the lawyer is something that your lawyer can do but that you must not. Asking the lawyer "why is that relevant?" or telling him that he's already asked that question and to move on to another one is the wrong thing to do. It puts you in the wrong frame of mind, it distracts you from the job you have at the deposition, and it may make you look bad and harm your credibility. Your job is simply to answer the questions, and let your lawyer argue with the other lawyer if that is needed. In addition, avoid the common temptation to ask yourself, "why is he asking me that?" Or, "where is he going with this line of questioning?" Or, "what is he going to say if I give this answer or that answer?" First, you never will figure out what the lawyer is thinking all of the time, and often, they are thinking a lot less than you suspect. More importantly, it is absolutely impossible to, at the same time, try to guess what the lawyer is thinking and where the lawyer is going, and simultaneously do what you are <u>supposed</u> to be doing which is focusing on: What is the question? What is the answer? When you try to do both at the same time, the result will simply be bad answers.

In addition to preparing you for your deposition, your lawyer must also prepare for the deposition of the witnesses who are friendly to your side. The extent to which your lawyer can meet with those witnesses ahead of time and prepare them for the process will depend on a variety of factors, both strategic and involving issues of privilege. Obviously, there is a real advantage when your lawyer believes that it is appropriate to meet with and prepare helpful witnesses before they testify. Good lawyering can have a very significant impact on how these witnesses perform as witnesses, which of course has itself a big impact on your chances of winning your case. The first critical key, as we have discussed before, is for your lawyer to tune in to these people as people. Each one is unique. They are probably not thrilled about the idea of giving testimony, and a variety of factors may turn them into good witnesses or bad witnesses.

Go back to how you graded this witness when you were doing your initial assessment. What is the role of this witness as a storyteller, and in the story? How credible is this witness? How likeable? How smart? How scared? How much instruction is this witness going to be able to absorb and retain in preparing for her role as a witness? Is there anything on the line in this case for this witness? Is it possible that she is afraid that she is going to be blamed for something, or that she's going to lose her job, or that someone is going to be angry with her? Does the witness have any personal motivations that may impact on his testimony? Managing witnesses and getting them emotionally and intellectually on track is a real skill, and separates good from mediocre lawyers. This is why most good trial lawyers are "people people," with strong people skills and an ability to connect to a wide variety of personalities.

Chapter 11

The Battle

What we can call the battle is simply the process of engaging your opponent to a result, to a partial or complete outcome in the case. The elements of battle, where the opposition is so engaged, are settlement negotiations and mediation, motions, and trial or appeal. Negotiations and motions can occur at any time in the process. Trial and appeal are the end game.

Books, movies, and television emphasize the oratorical skills of the lawyer, along with surprising and dramatic disclosures, as the key elements of this phase of litigation. Most of the time, however, equal or greater marquee status should be given to the foundations upon which this activity rests— proper factual and legal assessment, careful strategic planning, and skillful work in the investigation and discovery of the case.

When we explore how to win, we will see that in real lawsuits, there are many ways to win, and many points in the process where the case can be won. Winning is a harvest that usually results from seeds carefully sown. It is an outcome that usually results from numerous steps carefully taken to set up the victory. Winning sometimes is simply about one side beating the other, where, as in a sporting match, there is at the end of the day a clear winner and a clear loser. However, sometimes, the outcome is best described by the old and tired cliché "win win," where two parties to a dispute identify what they believe to be a resolution that best meets the needs of both sides.

The single most important fact that you need to understand about the role of lawyers in battle is this: it is not about us. It is about you. It is not about who is the greatest lawyer, it is not about our egos, it is not about win/loss records, and it is not about publicizing our wartime heroics. This battle results from a real dispute between real people, and in the end, it will result in a resolution of that dispute, one way or the other. The focus in fiction and in the media on the lawyers may make for better entertainment, but it creates a false impression. Our system of justice is just that, and if I try your case, you are going to live with the outcome of that lawsuit far longer than I do.

Reports of lawsuits always begin by telling you which lawyer won. Let us be direct. Each lawyer who got paid won. It is the parties to the dispute who can win or lose, not the lawyers. Winning and losing for lawyers is about ego, about bragging rights, and about marketing. Winning and losing for the parties is about a lot more, it's about why we have a system of justice to begin with.

As we prepare to discuss "winning," let us review the definition:

The Definition of Winning

Litigation is a problem-solving function. The lawyer is handed a series of cards (the facts, the evidence, and the witnesses) that cannot for the most part be changed. The goal (winning) is to play those cards to the best possible result. Results are measured by outcome and cost.

III.

WINNING

Chapter 12

Winning Before Trial

There are three significant opportunities to win a case before trial, to engage your opponent to a partial or complete outcome in your favor. One of these opportunities will be focused upon in the next chapter, the opportunity to win by settlement. The other two—winning in discovery and winning by motion, often go hand-in-hand.

Many cases are won or lost in the discovery and investigation process. As we have discussed, setting up your case properly by getting the information you need, asking the right questions, giving the right answers, obtaining and controlling the documents, controlling the witnesses, making proper use of experts, and developing your story—all of this sets up the checkmate you are looking for. In many cases, that partial or complete decisive blow comes in the form of a motion, such as a motion for summary judgment. The rules vary in different jurisdictions, but the general idea of a motion for summary judgment is that you ask the judge to rule that there is no reason to go to trial, because the other side has no case. These motions can be used to end an entire lawsuit (summary judgment) or to end a part of a lawsuit (summary adjudication). Here's how it works.

As we discussed before, in a jury trial, the judge decides what the law is as applied to your case, and the jury decides what happened factually, then applying the law as instructed by the judge. If you can convince the judge that there is no factual issue, that as a matter of law you win the case even under the facts as painted by the other side, then the judge can take the case away from the jury. This can happen by a pretrial motion, and it can also happen after the trial is over, in motions filed after the trial. Obviously, if it is possible to get such a ruling before an expensive and lengthy trial, you are better off.

The key to winning one of these motions, if you bring it, is to convince the judge that, no matter how one looks at the facts, you win. If you are opposing one of these motions, you must convince the judge that there are issues of fact that must be decided, and that if a jury sees the facts the way you do, a verdict in your favor would be consistent with the law.

So, how do you set one of these cases up? How do victories during the discovery phase of the case set up victories by motion, and provide the opportunity to win a case before trial? A case I handled some years ago provides a good illustration of how this can work. The case actually wound up being decided by the California Court of Appeal in a published decision which made new law in the area of summary judgments in the State of California. However, the more interesting part of the case is the story that it tells about the relationship between discovery and motions.

The plaintiffs had filed a 229-page complaint against 40 defendants, accusing them of fraud and conspiracy in connection with some complex transactions relating to the leasing of medical equipment. Boring stuff. My client, a bank, was probably the target defendant. Although the plaintiffs told a long and harrowing tale of evil, greed, and treachery that rivaled any Italian opera, we were quite convinced that their story was, to be kind, full of baloney.

Other defendants in the case generated a great deal of activity attacking the plaintiffs' pleadings, going to court repeatedly to argue about this and that, taking depositions, and organizing a boatload of documents. For our part, we did as little as possible, and kept a low profile. I then sent the plaintiffs a modest set of written discovery. I sent them requests for admissions, including the following: (1) "Admit that [my client] committed no fraud or deceit upon you"; and (2) "Admit that [my client] did not participate in any conspiracy to defraud you."

Along with these requests for admissions, I sent a set of interrogatories. The interrogatories asked the plaintiffs, for each request for admission that they had denied, to (1) state all facts upon which their denial was based; (2) identify all persons who had knowledge of any of the facts they were alleging; and (3) identify all documents that supported that response.

The plaintiffs could not admit my requests for admissions, because to do so would be to admit that they had no case against my client. So they denied them. Now they had to answer the interrogatories. The problem was, they apparently had no clue what my client had done wrong; as happens often in these big commercial cases, they simply knew that they had lost a large amount of money, believed it was someone else's fault, and had sued everybody in sight in the hopes of either shaking loose a good theory or shaking loose a generous settlement. So, in response to my interrogatories, they could only respond as follows: "Plaintiffs believe that [my client] knowingly and fraudulently took the assignment of all of the assets of [their client] to secure the loan it made. Plaintiffs reserve the right to further respond to this interrogatory." In simple English, they said that they believed we had done something wrong, but they didn't know what.

We then filed a motion for summary judgment, arguing that in an ordered universe, a plaintiff should know what you have done wrong before they sue you. In addition, <u>before</u> our motion could be decided, the plaintiffs had the right and opportunity to see all of our documents, and to take discovery from us. We correctly pointed out that, after all of this, they had nothing against us.

Many judges don't like to grant motions for summary judgment, particularly in complicated cases it's easier to let the jury sort it all out. Our judge denied the motion for summary judgment, probably for that reason. We took it to the Court of Appeal, and the Court of Appeal reversed the judge and ruled in our favor. The appellate decision stated in part:

> "Defendant contends that the factually devoid answers to the…interrogatories were sufficient to require the plaintiffs to prove their case concerning the alleged misrepresentations and fraudulent conspiracy. Defendant further argues that plaintiffs failed to provide substantial evidence of

misrepresentations or a conspiracy in the declarations and documents cited in their opposition…We agree."

Union Bank v. Superior Court, 31 Cal. App. 4th 573, 581 (1995).

This is just a simple example. Sometimes you can set up a fatal blow with one question in a deposition asked of the key plaintiff or the key defendant. Sometimes it is by generating that critical contradiction in their evidence, forcing them to disclose that poisonous document or email, or even by establishing that the evidence they seek to use against you is not legally admissible. Other times, it is by painstakingly establishing that their story doesn't stick, that there is no fire behind the smoke, that their dots do not connect or, as a great writer once said about a location she thought little of, "there is no there there."

When lawyers are not careful, thoughtful, and meticulous about the details of their case, they often miss opportunities to win cases early. Going back to what we have repeatedly discussed before, it is the accurate initial assessment of your lawsuit and the careful strategic planning of your lawsuit that will win the day far more often than courtroom dramatics and oratorical grandstanding. It is before trial that most great victories are quietly obtained.

Chapter 13

Winning by Settlement

Many people think of "winning" and "settlement" as inconsistent concepts. There is winning or losing, on one side, and settling on the other. If you are in a lawsuit, I suggest you think differently. Most cases do settle—that is how most lawsuits come to a conclusion. If your lawsuit ends by settlement, you want to win that settlement.

Winning a settlement is not just a function of being a good negotiator or a great poker player. In the movies, the great negotiator is portrayed like a crafty riverboat gambler, boldly demanding 20 times more for his claim than he knows it is worth, or coldly offering a small fraction of the reasonable value of the claim. Returning to our theme, the fact is that most well-negotiated settlements are built on the foundation of meticulous assessment, strategy, and set-up that precedes the negotiations. Having said that, however, there is certainly a real advantage in this process for those who are experienced and capable in the art of negotiating. I will never forget a negotiation I had early in my career with a young and inexperienced government attorney, who was bringing a claim for fines and penalties against my client. With too many cases on his desk, he called me up one day, and said the following: "Bob, I want to see if we can settle this case. Tell your clients that we are willing to settle all claims for $100,000, but if they won't pay $100,000, see if you can get them to agree to $75,000, and if you can't get that much, at least get back to me and let me know what they are willing to pay."

I will never forget that conversation, because the poor dear man did something that I had previously not been sure was possible; he actually bid against himself twice in one sentence. Although I personally liked this young lawyer very much, and putting aside whatever my client would have been prepared to do to settle the case before the conversation began, by the time he had finished his sentence, I was unfortunately not in a position to offer him $100,000 to settle the case, nor was I in a position to offer him $75,000. He had already told me that he would accept less. We settled the case promptly, and my client was very happy.

Indeed, an important part of negotiating is being schooled in the art of negotiating, and in the art of reading people and situations. However, in addition to this rather intangible aspect of the process, there are three key components to setting up your lawsuit for victory in settlement negotiations. Each of these three components is very important, and is something over which you do have tangible control, where doing it right can make a real difference. These are:

1. **Assessment;**
2. **Discipline; and**
3. **Managing the other side.**

The foundation for your efforts to obtain a good settlement is, first and foremost, a valid **assessment** of the case. Many cases settle after substantial discovery, motions, or even "on the courthouse steps" right before trial. An advantage to later settlement negotiations is that you approach them armed with a more sophisticated analysis of the case than is usually possible when you are seeking an early settlement. We discussed earlier the steps that must be taken in order to develop a good initial assessment of your lawsuit, early in the game. Later in the game, you are in a position to approach your assessment in an even more analytical way. A sophisticated final assessment of a case can take many forms; one of these forms is the **"decision tree"** approach, which is explained in some detail at the end of this chapter. The decision tree is based on multiple assessments of probabilities, and leads to a fairly detailed analytical framework for valuing a complicated case. The fact is that many cases will not require this kind of approach, but it is very useful to understand how it works in any event. Sometimes, even in what appears to be a simple case, it is a tool that can give you a sense of comfort about your conclusions of value. The decision tree model builds upon the assessments that must be made, no matter how you choose to approach this process: thorough and accurate assessments about the legal and factual issues in your case, the quality of your witnesses, the quality of your evidence, the cohesion of your story, the likeability and effectiveness of your storytellers and the same but flip side assessment of the other side's case. One way or another, you must arrive at a reliable assessment of the costs and risks inherent in your settlement position, and in your trial position.

Armed with a good assessment, you are ready for the next step in preparing yourself for a settlement victory: **facing reality** and **exercising self-discipline** in the face of that reality. Reality is not the same thing as fear. Facing reality does not mean looking at the situation too darkly, any more than with rose-tinted glasses. However, assessments that are polluted by bravado, fear, denial, or political considerations (particularly for companies) are often, in hindsight, the cause of bad settlements, or of missed opportunities at good settlements. Once you have a good assessment of your case, you need to believe in that assessment, to accept it, and to be disciplined about your negotiation strategy. Discipline, for example, is what often separates the better stockbrokers and investment advisors from the rest. It is hard enough to try to analyze or guess what the reasonable value of a stock is, at what price it is worth buying, and at what price it should be sold. However, the equally important, and even more difficult step, is exercising the discipline to put your assessment into action, to have the courage of your conviction and to actually sell that stock when it hits the price that your analysis told you should trigger a sale. Discipline is very important in negotiating. It is usually a process of many small steps, and every step must be taken in a disciplined and reasoned way.

Finally, settlement negotiations are about **managing** the other side, about doing everything you can to change their behavior and their thinking in ways that will help you get what you want. Making peace with the enemy usually requires a **viable line of communication**, and **reliable intelligence.** You may recall our earlier discussion about setting the tone for the case, and planning this process. The level of communications between your side and their side may have an important impact on the outcome of settlement discussions, and if your **strategic plan** has included posturing the case for settlement, you have hopefully been successful in controlling the tone of the case to this end. In some cases, this can mean that your lawyer has a very cordial and professional relationship with opposing counsel; in other cases, it may mean no more than simply not allowing the last door of civility to have slammed shut.

Knowing and understanding the opposition is also critical. Careful observation and assessment will often yield useful signs to help you decide <u>when</u> and <u>how</u> to approach settlement. You can often ascertain weaknesses in your opponent's negotiating position, by thinking the matter through from their perspective. There are many things to be looking for. Focus on two categories of factors in assessing your opponent, and in developing intelligence on your opponent: **weaknesses and needs**.

Look for signs of the following **weaknesses** in your opponent:

- **Fear**. This can take many forms, and be a fear of going to trial, or a fear of continuing with the process, or a fear of something that may happen as the litigation process continues. It also may be a fear of certain outcomes, no matter what the probabilities are. An 80% chance of stubbing your toe is not so bad, but a 1% chance of taking a bullet in the head may be an unacceptable risk.

- **Emotional exhaustion**. This exhaustion can be with the process of the lawsuit, or with how this problem is compounding your opponent's other life or business problems that are going on at the same time.

- **Running out of money**. This can result from the costs of the lawsuit itself, or again, simply how these costs tie in with other things that are going on in your opponent's life affecting his or her cash flow and financial position.

- **Lawyer/client feuding**. If you pick up these signals, and they are sometimes subtle and sometimes not, you can see if your opponent is not getting along with her lawyer anymore. This can range from open hostility to a simple a lack of comfort and rapport. An aloof or negative relationship between the other side and her lawyer can present an important opportunity. They may both want out of this thing.

- **A need to make the case go away**. Sometimes there are factors involving the other side's life or business where, in the context of everything they are dealing with, they really need this lawsuit to be behind them.

- **The need to focus on something else**. This may result not so much from the fact that this lawsuit is a negative for your opponent, but rather that he has something important or positive that he really needs to focus all of his attention on right now, and needs to get rid of the distraction.

- **Concerns regarding publicity or reputation**. This lawsuit may have implications for your opponent in terms of publicity or reputation that go well beyond the actual merits of the lawsuit itself or its dollar value.

- **Business or life plan**. Your opponent may be making plans in terms of his personal life (something as simple as moving to another state) or if your opponent is a business, there may be a business plan developing (like wanting to sell the business) that puts pressure on your opponent to want to resolve this lawsuit.

In addition to understanding the weaknesses in your opponent's negotiation position and the pressure points affecting his thinking, you must also assess your opponent's **needs**—the issues that he will bring to the table, knowingly or unknowingly, as "got to have" elements of a settlement.

- **Catharsis**. Understand that some plaintiffs need an opportunity to tell their side of the story, and to vent their emotions, before they are ready to settle at any price. Understand that, when facing a family member in a wrongful death case, this lawsuit represents their last emotional battle on behalf of their lost loved one; settlement will mean finally burying and letting go. They will need to be ready to do this, and you may need to help them get there. Your opponent's need for cathartic release may also be as simple as allowing them to tell you off, and tell you how they feel, and listening politely, perhaps even with compassion if appropriate.

- **Respect.** Although lawsuits are usually about money, in some cases, your opponent needs to feel respected in order to let go; if now is the time when you want them to let go, you'd better give them the respect they need.

- **Paying the lawyer.** I have successfully battled my inner cynical demons by putting this item third on the list. The fact is that many, many settlements are driven by this issue. Your opponent may need money now to settle up with the lawyer and end the bleeding. Your opponent may, on the other hand, need to pay you an amount that leaves him enough money to pay his lawyer as well. In personal injury cases or other cases where the lawyer is working on a contingency, settlements are often driven more by the lawyer's fee than by any other factor. Calculate the percentage of any settlement amount that will wind up becoming the lawyer's fee; there are numbers at which the lawyer can't permit the settlement to take place. Conversely, if the lawyer needs money now, getting an attractive fee now may push the lawyer to recommend a settlement that is not necessarily in his client's interest. This is another example of where timing can be important. Where the opponent has a contingency fee lawyer, also assess how important this case is to the overall portfolio of cases you suspect this lawyer is currently managing. How much time have they put into the case, and how much more time will they have to put into the case if it doesn't settle? Understand the lawyer's motivations as much as you understand your opposing party's motivations.

- **Confidentiality or secrecy.** In some cases, this can be an important need for the other side and thus an important card to play.

- **The time factor.** Your opponent may want to pay you, but need time to do it. On the other side, an injured plaintiff with long term medical needs or loss of employment may need security over time, and need a settlement that addresses not only short term financial needs, but includes a plan for long term issues. This can be addressed with, for example, a "structured settlement," which provides the plaintiff not only with cash now, but a guaranteed annuity providing future cash flow or periodic payments over a long period of time.

- **Non-monetary needs.** Some cases settle by offering things in addition to, or other than, money. Some business cases settle by entering into new contracts for more business. A bank can settle a case by offering the plaintiff a loan or line of credit that she might otherwise not qualify for, something that may have great value to that individual. Sometimes credit reports need to be cleared. I settled one significant lawsuit, believe it or not, with nothing more than a letter of apology. In other types of cases, agreements about intellectual property rights or future intellectual property rights can be more important than money. Look for non-monetary needs on the other side.

Managing the other side also requires assessing who, on the other side, is the real decision-maker. This can be less obvious in some cases than in others. Sometimes, your opponent will do whatever his lawyer recommends. In other cases, the lawyer has a client who is completely out of control, and that client will do whatever he wants to do, whether rational or irrational. Sometimes your opponent is getting very good legal advice, and sometimes they are getting lousy legal advice and very poor assessment of their case by their own counsel. Finally, other people, behind the scenes, may be driving your opponent's thinking during settlement negotiations. You may be in a negotiation with an employee who claims that he was wrongfully terminated, but pick up early in the process on the fact that he will not agree to any settlement until his wife tells him that it is a good deal. Parties often have family members or friends or other external sources that are impacting their thinking and decision-making. When you pick up on these signals, you can then make the most of that information, by tailoring your negotiations and your presentation of your position to meet the issues or to address the people who are really driving the decision-making on the other side of the table.

Another important weapon you should bring to the settlement battlefield is your credibility. Many lawyers understand the need to maintain their credibility with the judge, but overlook the importance of maintaining their credibility with opposing counsel. If you and your lawyer, acting together, have demonstrated wisdom, correct analysis, and understatement throughout the litigation process, this cannot help but to have a useful impact when you sit down to the final negotiations, and explain to your opponents why they must see things your way.

Using Mediators

We discussed the mediation process, and mediators, in Chapter 6. Using a good mediator can be very helpful, and is sometimes critical, to getting a good settlement. However, you need to use the mediation process correctly.

First, you have to have the right mediator. The good news is that, almost always, your lawyer will have the ability to participate in picking the mediator, and your lawyer must know who he is picking and why. It is best if the mediator is a known quantity, and is picked knowing what their mediation style is, and how they will conduct the mediation. Next, you must let the mediator play his role, but you must also control the process. At the end of the day, my attitude in mediation is that the mediator works for me. I want to direct what they are doing, and when they are doing it. I want to help them understand what is motivating the other side, and how to manipulate the other side in our direction. Using a professional mediator does not mean being more passive in the negotiation process. It simply means playing it differently.

Sometimes the most critical thing in picking a mediator is using a mediator that the other side will trust and defer to. This means that you have figured out who the real decision-maker on the other side is, and then you pick the right mediator to play to that audience. This can make the difference, for example, between using a retired judge and not using a retired judge. Sometimes you know that the entire mediation is going to be a game of poker, and you need a mediator who is good at that. Other times, you believe that a mediator may truly influence the assessment of the other side, with a real possibility that the mediator can get them to change their settlement position dramatically in your favor. Make the most of those opportunities.

Every mediator has one goal—to settle. This is true not only because it is their job, but because that is how they "win." In trying to convince people that they are good mediators and that they should be hired, they like to brag about the settlement percentage of cases that they mediate. "I settle 95% of the cases I get." Their "winning" record is their "settlement" record. This means, to put it bluntly, that they will settle the case over your dead body, if necessary. Their concern is not whether the settlement is fair, or in your favor. They just need to close the deal. This means in turn that they are looking for signs of weakness on both sides, and push against the weaker side of the table. Remembering this is important. Remember that when you are speaking with a mediator, you are negotiating with that mediator just as much as you would be negotiating if you were speaking directly to the opponent. The tone of the conversation may not sound like a negotiation, but it is a negotiation. You won't always disclose all of your thinking to the mediator, no matter how "confidential" that conversation is, and you will not always take at face value everything that the mediator tells you.

It is also helpful to have a sense for the dynamics of the mediation process. Most mediations of cases with any complexity to them will take a full day. If the process begins at 9:00 or 10:00 o'clock in the morning, you usually will not exchange any real offers or demands before the end of the morning, or the beginning of the afternoon. Serious offers and demands won't be exchanged until mid-afternoon. The process will begin accelerating rapidly towards the end of the afternoon. Make sure you have access to food and drink, as needed. Don't get worn out, and don't give up too quickly. What seems impossible at 1:30 in the afternoon often happens at 4:45 p.m.

The Decision Tree

So what is your case really worth? At what price should you be willing to give up your lawsuit and take a settlement? Or what amount should you be willing to pay in order to settle the case today and avoid future costs and risks? It all comes down to probabilities. The reason why it all comes down to probabilities is because, with almost any case, if you try it 10 times, you won't get the same result 10 times. There are a range of possible outcomes, and it is your best estimate of that range that gives you your final analysis as to the value of the case, or of its risks.

Some cases are easier to evaluate, and can be evaluated, more or less, in a couple of steps. If your insurance company is evaluating a car accident, and you hit the other car from behind at a stop sign, they're going to conclude that you are going to lose the case. If there is nothing extraordinary about the other side's injuries, which involve damage to the plaintiff's car and some medical bills, the insurance company will value the case by including all of the costs of repairing the other person's car, and multiplying their medical bills by a multiplier that their experience has shown them, in this particular jurisdiction, to reasonably approximate what a jury would give that person for the pain and suffering of having experienced that injury.

Many cases are far more difficult to assess. In those cases, trying to determine, in one step, whether you will win or lose, and what the dollar amount of a jury award might be, is a much tougher task. In those cases, the task is made easier, and more reliable, by breaking it down into smaller pieces.

With a decision tree, you basically take the question and break it down into many smaller questions, and then assign probabilities to those questions. The "tree" then makes the decision for you as to valuation. Once you understand how the tree works, you will see that it can really be developed in many different ways, and to suit many kinds of cases or problems. You will also see that you can give the tree as many "branches" as you want, and that if you do it correctly, you can increase the reliability of the analysis by adding more detailed "branches" to your tree.

Let me first illustrate this point. Suppose that you are a plaintiff who will ask a jury to vote in your favor and then award damages against a defendant. You could, on the one hand, begin by simply asking yourself "what are the probabilities that the jury will give me something, rather than nothing; in other words, vote for me and not the defendant?" On the other hand, you could break this question down into many smaller pieces. In order for the jury to vote in your favor, (1) the judge must first deny the defendant's motion for summary judgment; (2) the judge must decide whether or not to admit a critical piece of evidence, without which, your chances of winning are much lower; and (3) the jury must believe a critical storytelling witness of yours, a person who can tell a good story but also might be seriously impeached. You can "add branches" to your decision tree by assessing the probabilities of each of these separate factors going your way, or the other way.

Let's see how a decision tree works, in the big picture. The decision tree analysis set out at the end of this chapter is prepared assuming that you are a defendant, and that you are one of several defendants in a lawsuit. We are assuming in this case that, under the law that applies, the jury will have the option of deciding (a) that you have no responsibility for the plaintiff's injuries, or (b) that you have all of the responsibility for those injuries, or, alternatively, (c) that you have only a portion of the responsibility and that other defendants are also partially at fault and therefore partially responsible. All of this is analyzed in the first portion of the tree concerning actual damages. The second portion of the tree assesses punitive damages, and then combines the actual and punitive damage analysis together to form a total value of the case. We are assuming here that, under the applicable law, the jury will have the option of deciding whether or not punitive damages should be assessed against your client, to punish it for its behavior.

You and your lawyer have first assessed what the chances are that the jury will agree completely with you and give the plaintiff no recovery against you. Your lawyer has told you that if you try this case ten times, you will probably lose it eight out of ten times, at least in some amount. You have therefore assigned an 80% probability factor to the jury finding you negligent and therefore, at least in part, responsible and this is reflected in the top left hand portion of the tree.

Next, you discuss with your lawyer what is likely to occur when the jury compares your actions and responsibility with the action and responsibility of the other defendants. After a lot of thought and analysis, your lawyer tells you that his best estimate, if this case were to be tried to many different juries, is that half the time the juries would find you completely responsible for this accident, that 35% of the time they would find you 75% responsible (someone else being 25% responsible), and that 15% of the time they would find you only 50% responsible. Your lawyer has explained to you that this does not tell you what any one particular jury will do, but reflects his experience that if you try this case many times, some juries will see things more in your favor, and some less. The upper right hand portion of the decision tree reflects the estimates we have just made. We have now developed a probability that you will be found 100% liable at .40, by multiplying 80% (the probability that you will be found liable at all) by 50% (the probability that, if you are found liable, you will be assessed 100% of the responsibility). Using the same system of multiplication, we have determined that your chances of being found 75% responsible are .28, and that your chances of being found 50% responsible are .12.

The next question is how much. Your lawyer has considered a number of factors, including the range of jury verdicts for similar injuries in your jurisdiction. His best estimate is that 25% of the time the jury would award $6 million to the plaintiff, 50% of the time they would award $3.5 million, and 25% of the time they would award $1.5 million. In other words, some juries will agree with the plaintiff's expert on damages, some of the juries will agree with the defendant's expert, but more often the jury will agree to a number between the two.

The bottom half of the actual damages portion of the decision tree reflects these estimates. The risk of a $6 million award against you, when multiplied by the 25% chance that this will be the number the jury agrees to, results in a $600,000 risk representing the 40% of the time that the jury will find you 100% responsible for this damage, an additional $420,000 risk representing the 35% of the time that the jury will find you 75% responsible, and an additional $180,000 risk representing the probability that the jury will find you 50% responsible. The same calculations are made for a possible $3.5 million award, and a possible $1.5 million award. The total number of $2,900,000 represents a dollar valuation of the risk of actual damages in this lawsuit.

We next go to the second half of the tree. Your lawyer has concluded that, half the time, a jury will find it proper to award punitive damages against your client. This may be because, under the applicable legal standard, they will find that you were more than just negligent in allowing this accident to take place. Again, this is a case that you will lose eight out of 10 times. Given the actual damage award estimates and how angry a jury is likely to get when presented with the facts of this accident, your lawyer has estimated that, if punitive damages are awarded, 25% of the time that award will be in the range of $10 million, 50% of the time it will be in the range of $5 million, and 25% of the time it will be in the range of $2 million. The second half of the tree does the calculations, as in the same manner as previously explained and then adds the risk value of the actual damages to the risk value of punitive damages, to come to a total of $2,200,000. So your final decision tree number is $5,100,000. What does that mean? It means that if you are this defendant, and that if you do not like or can't afford risk (in other words, you are risk-adverse), you will probably jump at any opportunity to settle the case for less than that number. Such a settlement eliminates all future costs of going forward (paying your lawyer, and all of the other expenses for experts and the legal process), and you have eliminated the risk that you wind up with a judgment against you of $16 million or more—which represents the "worst case scenario" in your assumptions of both actual and punitive damages. If you want to give yourself a more accurate risk number for the litigation, you need to estimate all of your legal and other costs of the case going forward through trial and appeal, and add those to the risk number provided to you by the tree. If there is a legal possibility that you may also be responsible for the attorneys' fees of the other side, as a result of statute or a provision in a contract, then you must factor that in as well.

Now, if you are the plaintiff in this story, and have generated the same decision tree, the "risk" number is really for you, an "opportunity" number, and you are looking for a settlement that is at least as high or higher.

Decision Tree Analysis
Mad vs. Client

Actual Damages

Assumptions:

1. Client will be found liable 8 out of 10 times the case is tried.
2. If Client is found liable, 50% of the time its liability will be assessed at 100%, 35% of the time its liability will be assessed at 75%, and 15% of the time its liability will be assessed at 50%.
3. 25% of the time a damage award will be $6 million, 50% of the time a damage award will be $3.5 million, and 25% of the time a damage award will be $1.5 million.

	(.40) 100% (50%)
80% Negligent	(.28) 75% (35%)
	(.12) 50% (15%)
20% No Negligence- No recovery by plaintiff	

	X .40	X .28	X .12
$6M (25%)	$600,000	$420,000	$180,000
3.5M (50%)	$700,000	$490,000	$210,000
$1.5M (25%)	$150,000	$105,000	$45,000
	$1,450,000	$1,015,000	$435,000

$2,900,000

Punitive Damages

1. Client will be found liable 8 out of 10 times the case is tried.
2. If Client is found liable, 50% of the time it will be found subject to punitive damages.
3. 25% of the time a punitive damage award will be $10 million, 50% of the time it will be $5 million, and 25% of the time it will be $2 million.

80% Neg on Client	(.40) 50% Punitive Damages Assessed
	50% No Punitive Damages Assessed
20% No Neg- No recovery by plaintiff	

$$X\ .40$$

$10M (25%)	=	$1,000,000
$ 5M (50%)	=	$1,000,000
$ 2M (25%)	=	$ 200,000
		$2,200,000

TOTAL DAMAGES: $2,900,000 + $2,200,000 = $5,100,000

Chapter 14

Winning at Trial

The impression many people have, both from entertainment and from the news, is that winning at trial is mostly about courtroom theater. It is about which side has, as its trial lawyer, the best dramatic actor. It is about the great soft shoe, and the great cross-examination. As the trial lawyer in the wonderful Broadway musical *Chicago* sings, "you've got to razzle-dazzle them."

Is that what winning trials is really all about? Well, to some extent, it is. It is absolutely true that there is no substitute for the skills that make some trial lawyers great storytellers, great at unraveling witnesses during cross-examination, and great at connecting with a jury both emotionally and intellectually. These factors are very real, and make a real difference in many cases. However, don't kid yourself that winning at trial is about having the best flimflam artist on your side. That false impression can only come from a mistake you never want to make—insulting the intelligence of juries. While it is true that some juries will do some really stupid things, most of the time they take their job very seriously and approach it very carefully. Insult their intelligence at your peril. Most juries are pretty good at separating the skills of the lawyer from the truth of the case, and any experienced trial lawyer or jury consultant will tell you that it is fairly common, when juries are interviewed after a trial, for jurors to report that they thought one side's lawyer was a much better lawyer, but that they believed the other side's story.

I think that most judges, trial lawyers, and trial consultants would agree that our trial system works fairly well, even though it is far from perfect. This means, by necessity, that it is not just about smoke and mirrors, or about who hires the best salesman. It means that, thankfully, one of the most significant factors that will determine whether you win your trial is whether you are right. It is hard for human beings to be objective about this sort of thing, and we all tend to believe, in every argument that we get into, that we are right. For many people in lawsuits, having a good lawyer and going through the discovery process helps them to take a reality check on their case, and is part of the reason most cases do in fact settle. However, if a case goes to trial, we must take a step back from analyzing all of the factors that go into winning a case long enough to accept the fact that, no matter what the lawyers on both sides do, the actual merits of the dispute will have a big part to play in who wins. Thankfully. Having said that, the next important point is that what you and your lawyer can do to improve your chances of winning a trial goes well beyond your lawyer's dramatic skills, as important as they may be. There are some other very important pieces of the puzzle, pieces which probably have a bigger part to play in "winning," in most cases, than Oscar-worthy performances by trial counsel.

Preparation

As we have developed in the previous chapters, putting yourself in a position to win the trial is something that has been carefully set up by doing a lot of things right, and very thoughtfully, in the months and years before the trial begins. Lawyers who go to trial regularly will tell you that some cases can be so well prepared and set up for victory that, in the courtroom, the case practically tries itself. It is simply a function of laying out the pieces of the puzzle that have been carefully built in advance. Experienced trial lawyers will also tell you stories of cases that they were asked to step into at the last minutes, cases that should have been easy to try and win if properly prepared, and that are now practically unwinnable because of the bad work or lack of work done before the trial started.

As we discussed in Chapter 2, a trial is a story. What actually happened in the dispute between the parties does not matter; what matters is what the jury is <u>told</u> about what happened. These two can be very different. Your story is often only as good as your weakest storyteller, just like a chain is as strong as its weakest link. If you don't have good storytellers who are available, lined up, and properly prepared to tell your story, you may not have a story to tell. In addition, because the trial is a theatrical re-creation by your lawyer of the events that led up to the lawsuit, your lawyer must have proper evidence and good evidence to tell your story. If key evidence has not been found, or cannot be admitted under the rules of evidence, you are in trouble.

Trial is where the big and little mistakes made in the

planning process, the investigation process, the discovery process, and the motion process really come back to haunt you. Or, hopefully, it is where they come back to haunt the other side. Some kinds of mistakes can be made by very intelligent and capable lawyers. A great example of this is in complex business litigation, in the big disputes between big business involving a great deal of money. Because the people involved in those kinds of cases have a lot of money, they can afford to hire the best lawyers, and they do. However, one of the interesting ironies of these cases comes from the fact that very few big, complex business cases actually go to trial. These are cases involving large amounts of paper, many witnesses, and therefore generating a great deal of legal activity—but rarely going to trial. This means that the most expensive law firms have armies of lawyers who spend their careers working on these big cases, many of whom never have even seen, let alone conducted, a trial. They don't understand the end game. Because of this, they can make many little mistakes in the pretrial process, mistakes that they don't recognize to be mistakes, because they don't understand how what they are doing can be used against them in front of a jury. For example, they may not appreciate the fact that being nasty or sarcastic while examining a witness in a deposition, or in written responses to interrogatories, can really make their client look bad if the jury hears or sees what they said.

Everything that has happened before the trial starts is part of what will unfold to the jury during the theatrical re-creation of your case at trial. Great movies begin with a great script, and great trial results begin with great preparation.

Picking a Jury

As we discussed in Chapter 2, depending upon what your dispute is about and who you are, there are some jurors who will be great for you, and some who will be terrible for you. Thus, as the beginning of the trial, one of the first and most critical steps is the process of jury selection. Although we tend to talk about "picking" a jury, we actually "unpick" a jury. Under the court rules, your lawyer does not get to choose who will be on the jury. Rather, a pool of possible jurors will be brought into the courtroom, and each side will be allowed to reject a limited number of those people. Although the rules are different in different jurisdictions, your lawyer will have a limited number of "bullets," or challenges to individual jurors that he can exercise. The decision as to who to challenge from this group of citizens presented to you for jury service is a very important decision, with important consequences. Some people, because of their life experiences, will tend to see things in a way that can be very bad for your case, that makes it quite unlikely that they will like you or believe your story. The most dangerous juror is a juror who is likely not to like you or your story, and who is likely to play an important role in the jury deliberations, because of the force of the juror's personality or for some other reason. Therefore, when you are assessing a potential juror, you are looking for two things: is this a "bad" juror, and if so, is this juror also a person who is likely to take a leadership position in the jury deliberations. The combination is poison, and these are the people who must get your first bullets.

Many trial lawyers think that they are good at picking or unpicking juries, and this belief usually flows from a healthy combination of insight, experience, and self-delusion. There are many approaches to this process, and different lawyers have found success using different techniques. You get three types of information about a potential juror, in trying to decide whether or not you should reject him. Again, the amount and nature of this information will vary greatly from jurisdiction to jurisdiction, and courtroom to courtroom. In general, you will usually get some written background information on the juror, and you will sometimes even be able to provide written questions to the members of the jury pool that they will answer in writing. Next, there is the process called "*voir dire*," where the juror is asked questions. Sometimes, only the judge asks questions; more often, the lawyers are allowed to ask questions as well, sometimes in a very limited way, and sometimes at length. In any event, you get to hear the answers to those questions. A third piece of information you get is by observation, by watching the potential jurors, by seeing whether they are interested or bored, alert or distracted, neatly dressed or sloppy, enthusiastic about being a juror or angry at being called, paying attention to what is being said or not, understanding questions or not, etc.

Some lawyers will rely very heavily on their gut feeling about whether a particular juror is connecting with them and their client during this *voir dire* process. Other lawyers will have developed a list of factors that they are looking for, characteristics that they believe will exist in a juror who is likely to side with them, and characteristics of "bad" jurors. Someone who has had bad experiences with police officers may be expected not to believe the testimony of police officers. An engineer may be expected to really hold the plaintiff to the burden of proving what he is alleging fairly clearly, and to proving his damage calculations carefully. A creative or artistic personality may be expected to be more likely to buy into a conspiracy theory that is only loosely developed with hard evidence, perhaps because their imagination will connect dots that are otherwise not all that well-connected. People who have had problems with insurance companies will be more sympathetic to claims by someone who is having such a problem. People who have been victims of violent crime will probably respond strongly to a case involving an allegation of violence.

With any case, the lawyer can make lists of factors that should be considered in judging a potential juror. The lawyer can also consider bigger questions; if your case is going to involve a lot of boring documents and complicated facts, you want to take a hard look at the attention span of potential jurors, and their general interest level in following the proceedings. You may need jurors who will pay attention, or, conversely, you may love the juror who "spaces out" in a matter of minutes. In considering all of these factors, remember two things. First, at its very best, what you are doing is guesswork. You are trying to guess about people based upon very little information, and you will often get it wrong. Second, you are trying to draw conclusions from one piece of information about this person, but doing so without the context of all of the other relevant information that you may not have. The criminal defense attorney may love the fact that a young woman is very liberal, and does not think highly of police officers. But depending upon the nature of the crime he is defending, if he doesn't also find out that this young woman was herself a rape victim, he may be in for a big surprise. Another example of where what seems at the surface to be simple may be more complicated is with school teachers. The third grade teacher may seem very liberal, very sympathetic to the socio-economics of a criminal defendant, and very untrusting of the criminal justice system. These factors would suggest that she is a good "defense" juror in a criminal case. But don't forget that this same school teacher, when the trial is over, must return to her third grade classroom, and tell the children whether she voted to send a criminal to prison, or to let him go. Uh, oh, not so simple.

So, how does one sort out all of these contradictions, and take the best shot possible at this jury selection process. The answer is that you will, at best, always be dealing with guesswork; however, the more information you have, and the more sources of information you have, the better your guesses are likely to be. In some cases, this simply means having a trial lawyer who is experienced at jury selection, and has given a lot of thought to exactly what the lawyer is looking for, and not looking for, in your particular case. In some cases, it will mean also obtaining the services of a jury consultant. Jury consultants are expensive, and can only be used in cases where that expense makes sense. However, good jury consultants can be quite helpful with the process of selecting a jury, as well as with the process of deciding what kinds of arguments will and will not work with certain kinds of jurors, in your particular case. There are different things that jury consultants can do, and do do. Three of the most common are sitting with the lawyer at jury selection, conducting jury surveys, and conducting mock trials. The first of these is where the consultant sits in the courtroom with you and your lawyer during the jury selection process. The consultant may have assisted in developing the questions that will be asked of the potential jurors, and the consultant observes responses and behavior, then provides advice as to which jurors should be rejected. The other two principal functions of jury consultants are, in my view, more analytical and more interesting. In conducting jury surveys, what the consultant does is to identify the population from which the jury pool will be selected for the courthouse where you will be trying your case. Then, using standard marketing tools, they develop a randomly selected pool from that community, which is demographically balanced in terms of age, gender, income level, and other relevant factors. The most common way of doing this is in the form of a telephone survey, and the people who respond may be offered some payment for their time. The people are asked a series of questions, some of which are to determine background demographic information, and some of which are designed to test their attitudes about issues in your case. You can then find out two things: (1) how people, in general, are reacting to issues in your case; and (2) what individual characteristics in these people tend to predict whether they will be for you or against you. For example, you may find that men and women are reacting differently to a key issue in your case, or that there are such differences between people with more or less money, more or less education, people who are younger or older, etc. So, to give a simplistic example, you may conclude that older women who are well educated are very bad jurors for you. However, the information you obtain may be far more specific, and far more helpful than even that.

I once had a case where the client I represented was well-known and extremely unpopular. There wasn't any question about the fact that the jury was going to react negatively to who my client was. I hired a jury consultant in that case to conduct a telephone survey. The survey revealed two things that were very helpful to me in trying the case. First, although the survey confirmed the negative attitude about my client, it also gave me very specific information about exactly what it was about my client that generated the most negative reactions. Second, part of my case involved an employment relationship, where my client was the employer. We know that, generally speaking, juries are far more sympathetic to the employee than to the employer, because the typical juror empathizes far more with the position of the employee. The surprise to me, coming out of the survey, was that notwithstanding the very strong negative feelings that people had in general about my client, my client's role as an employer was still going to be a larger hurdle for me to overcome than simply who my client was. Having reviewed the results of the survey, I not only changed my *voir dire* questions, but

I completely rewrote my opening statement to the jury. What changed was what I chose to emphasize, and what I chose to play down.

Another important fact that can be discovered in jury surveys is what other factors or events are currently impacting on how juries think about the issues which you will be presenting in your trial. By knowing what they are thinking, and how they are thinking, you can better approach your presentation. Sometimes, you can find out about these things and address them; other times, they are completely out of your control. In one of my cases, the jury had to determine the cause of death of a patient in a nursing home. The question was whether the patient had died of natural causes, or whether wrongdoing by nurses or the doctor had contributed to the patient's death. Much was at stake, because if the jury came out the wrong way, the doctor was likely to be criminally prosecuted. As luck would have it, the week that we were trying this case, the local affiliate of one of the major broadcast networks was running, on the local evening news, a week-long series entitled "Warehouses of Neglect." It was about nursing homes. After the trial was over and while the jury was deliberating, the courtroom bailiff told me confidentially (always be on good terms with all of the courtroom employees!) that the jury, in its deliberations, spent over an hour talking just about that television show. This is a great example of factors totally outside of the facts of your case which can have an important part to play in the jury's decision.

Another important tool of jury consultants is what are called mock trials. There are different forms of mock trials, but the general idea is that you start with a pool of people who represent the jury you are likely to get, and then do a very short "mock trial" to those people, getting their reactions. Again, standard marketing techniques are used to identify people who come from the community where your jury pool is likely to be drawn from, and who represent a cross-section of that community. They are offered payment in return for a day or an evening of their time. They are typically told ahead of time only that they are participating in market research. The information you obtain from this process can be very detailed, and very revealing. Again, it's not cheap to do this.

We conducted a mock trial in connection with a case that was legally very simple and factually very complicated. Our client was a bank, and the allegations involved several customers, and stories that were truly hard to believe. The problem was that there was no version of this story, no scenario, that wasn't almost as equally unbelievable as the others. The great puzzle for us was, what was the jury likely to believe, and why?

Our jury consultant developed a pool of 24 "jurors," representing a cross-section of the jury pool we would be receiving from the courthouse. They were paid for an afternoon and evening of their time, and we made a presentation to them. After that presentation, they were divided into three juries of eight. At the beginning, based upon a questionnaire that they filled out, each juror was identified in terms of sex, race, age, family income, education, etc. They were also identified in terms of a number of general factors, including their experience with religion, lawsuits, problems with banks, and opinions about certain background issues. Our presentation involved one lawyer making an opening statement and closing argument for the plaintiff, and a different lawyer making an opening and closing argument for the defendant. In addition to summaries of the evidence and testimony given by the lawyers, the jurors watched portions of the videotaped depositions of some of the key witnesses, or storytellers in the case. While the presentations were taking place, each juror had in his or her hand a dial, which they turned to the left when they were reacting negatively to something, and to the right when they were reacting positively to something. A videotape and computer then provided us with a real time reaction by each of the jurors to every part of every argument made, and to every part of the videotaped deposition testimony that they watched. We saw and recorded how people were reacting in general, but could also break it down to see how men were reacting, how women were reacting, how well-educated people were reacting, etc.—all categorized by the demographic and background information issues we had identified for each juror. We now had very detailed information as to which arguments worked, and which arguments flopped, for each side. We also saw which witnesses did well, and which part of their testimony did well or badly, and with whom.

Next, the jurors were divided into three separate juries, to deliberate. Each group deliberated in a separate room, each room having a one-way mirror behind which we watched and videotaped what was going on. We saw how each of the three juries came to their decision, and which jurors took leadership roles and drove the decision.

The results of all of this information were quite remarkable, and frankly dramatically changed our attitude about our case, as well as about how we would pick a jury, and what arguments we would emphasize. One of our key motivations in doing the mock trial in this case had been to show the client, who had key representatives attend and participate in the process, just how difficult the case was and how dangerous the case was. What the mock trials told us was that the case was far more winnable than we had suspected, and it provided us with very useful information on how we could increase our chances of winning. Information obtained from mock trials and jury surveys also serves a more modest but equally useful purpose, simply in terms of validating things that you suspect to be true. For example, in our mock trial, there were aspects of some of the plaintiff's testimony that we did not believe, and that we did not believe a jury would find credible. It was one thing to come to this conclusion on our own. It was quite another to watch a roomful of prospective jurors literally exploding into laughter as they watched that videotaped testimony actually being given by those witnesses.

Equally important, the mock trial identified some very specific types of personalities that were absolute poison for us, that, if left on the jury, would move heaven and earth to hurt our case. As we have discussed before, this is the single-most important factor to identify in preparing to select your jury.

Winning the Evidence Wars

As we have discussed, the only part of your story or the other side's story that will matter at all is the part that the jury hears. Many an unprepared lawyer has shown up for trial, eager to begin crying his tale of heartbreak to the jury, only to have the judge rule, right before the trial starts, that most of his "evidence" is inadmissible and will not see the light of day in front of the jury. Before the jury hears any evidence, or any testimony, each side has the opportunity to ask the judge to decide whether some particular item of evidence or testimony should be excluded, under the rules of evidence. When these motions are made at the very beginning of the trial, they are called motions in limine. These decisions are made by the judge based upon his or her interpretation of evidence law.

Two things are important to understand about evidence law. The first is that it can be mind-numbingly complicated, beyond what common sense would suggest. It is one of the areas of law that law students tend to find the most confusing, and it is certainly one of the areas of law that, after having gotten an A in the "evidence" course in law school and after having passed the bar exam, they understand the least about. Applying the rules of evidence in law school hypotheticals and applying them in a courtroom in a real life situation is a very different experience indeed. The second thing you need to understand about the rules of evidence is that, to call them "rules," may be charitable. In truth, different judges will rule very differently on the same evidentiary questions, and so no matter how well-schooled your lawyer is in the law of evidence, it will be very difficult for him to predict how the judge will rule on many of the evidence issues that are coming up in your case. This is one of the great aspects of uncertainty in a trial, and can be very frustrating but must be accepted for what it is.

What a good lawyer does, well before trial, is two things in terms of the evidence. First, the lawyer makes absolutely sure that all of the evidence that he needs to get before the jury has been set up, to the best possible extent, to be admissible and safe from any attempt by the other side to have it excluded. Next, the lawyer makes a list of all of the items of evidence that hurt your side of the case, and tries to come up with the best possible argument for having it excluded. This includes all the documents (or portions of documents) that are unhelpful, as well as all of the testimony. Then, before the trial, the lawyer files motions in limine, laying out all of the legal arguments to the judge as to why that evidence should be excluded. If the judge excludes the evidence, this means that the lawyer on the other side will be barred from making any reference about that material to the jury, and will be ordered to instruct every witness that he puts on the witness stand, in advance, that they may not make any reference to that evidence either. To violate that order is potentially a contempt of court, and cause for a mistrial.

You have probably seen very few movies or television shows containing dramatic scenes of lawyers arguing motions in limine. However, many trials are set in a completely new direction by successful motions to exclude evidence. Moreover, a lawyer that truly understands the rules of evidence and pays attention to them can really change the course of a trial. I once tried a case involving a major criminal fraud. The plaintiff in our case was pretending to have been a victim of the criminal activity, when we believed that she was in fact a part of that criminal activity. The FBI had in fact a tape recording of the plaintiff. They had confronted one of the criminal conspirators, who was going to be prosecuted, and convinced her to cooperate. That individual had then been wired, and had lured the plaintiff into an underground parking garage to have a conversation about their crime. When I interviewed the FBI about this wired conversation, they told me that it was unusable, and that they had not been able to prosecute as a result. There was so much loud traffic in the parking area at the time of the conversation that the speech could not be heard. The FBI gave me the original tape, for what it was worth.

I took that tape to a sound specialist. Working long and hard with very sophisticated equipment, my expert was able to clean the tape up, making successive generations of tape as he cleaned different parts of the noise and background sound. After many such generations of cleaning, we had a tape where you could hear the conversation. It was slow, it was muffled, but you could hear it distinctly; the plaintiff was admitting that she was a criminal.

I played that tape for the jury. Before I played that tape for the jury, two unfortunate things took place. The unfortunate thing for me was that my sound expert, in the final process of cleaning the original FBI tape, inadvertently destroyed it. It was physically ruined, and could not be played. The unfortunate thing for my opponent was that he did not challenge the "foundation" (one of those mind-numbing evidentiary principles) of the final generation tape that I <u>did</u> play for the jury. Had he made an evidentiary challenge to the foundation of that tape, the jury might never have heard it. I must admit that I enjoyed watching the plaintiff's face as she listened, along with the jury, to her recorded words for the first time.

Sometimes an evidentiary motion is to keep out of evidence some very bad facts which are legally inadmissible, but which would dramatically change how the jury sees the case. One of my cases relied, importantly, on the testimony of a former senior executive of my client company. His testimony was honest and straightforward, and he was a key storyteller. He testified well at trial. Fortunately for me, I was able to convince the judge that the jury should not be allowed to hear the fact that he had been fired from the company for embezzlement, having embezzled money for the purpose of supporting his cocaine habit, for which he had spent time in federal prison. Those facts were all truly unrelated to what he was testifying about, or to whether he should be believed as to what he was testifying about. Nevertheless, you can imagine that it wouldn't have helped my case if the jury had heard it.

Managing Your Storytellers

We have talked about the critical importance of your storytellers, and of the steps that must be taken, before trial, to manage those storytellers and manage their role in the case. In order to be helpful at trial, your storytellers must (1) show up; (2) perform well; and (3) not completely contradict what they said in their prior testimony, for example at a deposition. None of this happens by itself, and because your storytellers are people, managing them is a dynamic process.

Witness management is one of the parts of lawyering that really tests the people skills of your lawyer. Witnesses present many different kinds of problems, including last minutes changes in attitude about testifying right before trial. Managing those problems as best as possible is critical. A witness who may have been very supportive throughout the pretrial process may get cold feet right before trial. That witness may also suddenly, for some other reason, decide that they don't like you very much anymore. Companies often have employee witnesses who leave their employment shortly before trial, and suddenly have a very different attitude about helping out the company. Witnesses can become terrified at the prospect of testifying in open court, or they may become so combative that they lose their credibility.

In terms of managing the emotions of a friendly witness, your lawyer has far less control during trial than he does during a deposition. At a deposition, your lawyer may be able to spend a long period of time getting the witness into the right frame of mind, right before the testimony begins. Then, there are regular bathroom breaks, rest breaks, and meal breaks during the deposition process, all giving your lawyer an opportunity to get the witness back on track if necessary. Little or none of this is available at trial. If one of your key witnesses is testifying in the third day of the trial, there will be little or no opportunity to interact much with that witness right before he takes the witness stand. Once on the witness stand, there will be no opportunity to coach or assist him until the testimony is over.

I once had a witness, the former head of security for a large company, who was a critical storyteller in our case. He was an elderly gentleman with a very strong personality. He was honest as the day is long, and had a good heart, but could easily come off as a curmudgeon. If pushed into an argument, he could become downright ornery. The problem for me was that the other side was trying to portray my client as uncaring and mean-spirited; any success in making this witness look nasty or feisty was going to hurt my case.

In preparing this witness during the two years before he testified at trial, I discussed this issue with him openly and repeatedly. I told him that it would be important at trial for his real personality to come through. I explained to him that he could come off as gruff under the wrong circumstances, and that someone who did not know him might interpret that gruffness as a mean streak. I wanted the jury to see him for who he really was inside. The contrast I painted for him was between being a mean old man and being a grandfather. I wanted him to be a grandfather. I repeatedly drilled that image into him before we went to trial.

At trial, as is typical, I was not able to speak to this witness for several days before the day he testified. One of my assistants made the arrangements for him to be at the courthouse on the day of his testimony, and because the length of testimony is always unpredictable, he wound up sitting in the courthouse hallway for two or three hours before it was his turn to testify. My only contact with him before he took the witness stand was, after the judge had barked "Call your next witness," and I walked out into the hallway to bring him into the courtroom. As I walked out of the court and brought him in, I put my arm around his shoulders, and whispered into his ear, "okay, grandpa, let's go." It worked. They didn't lay a glove on him.

Showing Your Story

As we discussed in Chapter 2, perhaps the most important part of telling your story is showing your story. This is the art of **visualization**. There are several reasons why visualization is so important. First, people remember far more from seeing things than from hearing them. Second, you can't bore your audience, and just talking to people gets boring very quickly, almost no matter what it is that you are talking about. Seeing is believing, and to entertain your audience is to keep it.

Helping the jury see your story is, in part, the careful use of language in your storytelling to create visual images in the mind's eye of the jury; it is also, in part, literally showing your story through illustrations, visual imagery, graphics, and other displays. Helping the jury to visualize your story comes from two important tools that must come together and work together; the first is the **visual** themes that you have pounded into the witness' testimony, the written discovery responses, and other forms of evidence that the jury will hear repeatedly, combined with the storytelling ability of your lawyer and your key storytellers. When these tools work together successfully, the jury will feel your pain, it will hear the cries in the night, it will see the flash of the gun, it will wince at the heartless response from the corporate giant, it will reel from the snarling dog...you get the point. Again, these tools are most effective when they are not simply invented on the spot at trial, but are reinforced by the seeds sown in other forms of evidence that the jury will hear, reinforcing your **themes** and **theory** of the case.

In terms of graphics and visual evidence, the role of these tools just continues to expand in the modern trial. Technology makes new and more dramatic tools available to trial lawyers every year, to the point where one of the factors you must pay attention to is overdoing it. With technology, sometimes a little goes a long way. Moreover, you have to mix it up, and any effective visual tool is best used by combining it with other visual tools. In other words, if there are a lot of things that you want to show the jury, it is best if you don't show them five days of Power Point presentations, or three days of movies, or 75 blown-up color charts, or 200 blown-up documents. If your case involves just a few visual presentations, pick one or two forms of presentation, and use them crisply. If you have to show a lot of things to the jury, then use different visual tools, and mix them up, moving from one to the other, so that things are changing with regularity. The cadence and dynamics of your overall presentation to the jury are as important as the cadence and dynamics of your voice when you are speaking to the jury. If your lawyer is speaking to the jury for half an hour, and remains during that entire time on the same note, or at the same volume, the presentation will be ineffective. A good speaker is changing pitch, changing volume, and changing speed of presentation with some regularity, even if in subtle ways, to keep things moving and changing and to keep the audience's attention. The overall dramatic presentation, the overall theatrical production of your story to the jury, has to have the same level of control in its presentation.

Good graphic artists and litigation support experts can make a real difference in the trial presentation. They have expertise that your lawyer probably does not have, in creating visual images to tell a story. In complicated cases, they can come up with some very interesting, creative, and entertaining ideas for how to convey details, often boring details, to a jury so that those details will be understood and absorbed. One simple example is the difference between standing in front of a jury and telling them what the profit numbers were for each quarter of every year for a company over a period of years, as opposed to showing them a colorful graph which is large enough to easily see, which is designed to be easily followed, and which shows how the company's profits continued to increase month after month and year after year. So, when that company continues to whine about how your client hurt their profits, you keep on throwing up that graph and saying "Yeah, where?"

Graphics are particularly important with material that is hard to understand or mind-numbingly dull. Take for example a case of mine involving allegations that a local government agency misused federal funds. The question involved an analysis of generally accepted accounting rules applicable to government, the tracing of sources of governmental expenditures, the rules concerning the expenditure of restricted federal funds, and how all of those rules were implemented by a particular government agency in connection with certain projects. No offense to my client, but you just can't get any duller than that. I don't care if you are P.T. Barnum or Franklin Roosevelt, but there is no way just to stand in front of a jury of ordinary citizens and talk about this stuff in a way that will keep their attention, keep them interested, or get them to understand what on earth it is you are trying to say. It is hopeless.

At the end of all of the drivel, the simple point that our expert was going to try to make was that the money spent by our client had not been restricted federal money, but its own money. Although the money had come from the federal government, it had gone into our bank account and become mixed up with money coming from other places, lost its "restrictions," and become our money to use as we pleased. The color of the money had changed from their color to our color. Our expert did a good job of explaining this, although not quite as glibly. But our graphic artist produced this large and beautiful graphic, showing stacks of money, in different colors, going into a pot. As they moved through the pot, the stacks changed color. The money going to the projects that were the subject of our lawsuit were a different color than the money coming from the federal government. It worked beautifully, it was a pleasure to look at, and anyone could understand it in a few moments.

In another case, I was representing the defendant in a case where the plaintiff was very, very sympathetic, and his story was heartbreaking. It really was. But the part where my client was responsible for that heartbreak just wasn't true, and there were several critical details in the story that the plaintiff had told repeatedly, but never consistently. He had spoken to the police, he had spoken to government investigators, he had spoken to friends, and he had given a deposition. Each time the story was a little different. At the end of the trial, I had to hammer that point home, because without it, the risk was that the jury would be caught up in the emotion of the story itself, and not focus on my client's lack of responsibility. A graphic artist prepared a superb graphic board, which I placed before the jury during my closing argument. Using color and design, the graphic set out each version of the witness' own words on what had happened concerning these critical details, showing how different they were, and showing how what he had told the jury at trial was totally inconsistent with his prior repeated statements to many people. The board had a large heading, at the top, "The Contradictions of Mr. Smith" (the name is obviously changed). The jury was mesmerized by that board, and each of them studied it meticulously and the lawyers presented their final arguments, and before they began their deliberations. That board drove the discussion in the deliberations, and that is what we wanted.

Unraveling Their Story

Everyone's favorite moment in trial is cross-examination. This is one of those rare moments when the movie and television lawyers are on the same page with the real trial lawyers; <u>everybody</u> loves cross-examination. It can be the most entertaining part of the trial, and for the trial lawyer, it can be the most fun part of the trial. A good lawyer can score at least some points with almost any witness, on any subject. There is usually some aspect of the story that can be made unclear, or be made to appear contradictory with other evidence or other stories told; there is always some question about how clear the witness is, or how sure she is, or how reliable her memory is. With the right opening, questions can be raised about the credibility of the witness, and their motivations for saying what they have said. Your lawyer must be careful with all of this, because it is a bit of a minefield. Cross-examination can blow up in your face if the jury thinks you are being unfair, too clever, too mean, or beating up the witness on issues that they think are unimportant. Also, as has been said so many times before, you must really, really know where you are going. I once watched a lawyer cross-examine my forgery expert. He was an elderly gentleman who was considered, perhaps, the foremost forgery expert in the world. He had testified thousands of times and been involved in many high-profile and famous cases. He was the Moses of forgery. After hearing his background, and during his entire presentation, the jury had been eating out of his hands. His point was that a stamp placed on a document by a teller had been made with a stamp that was forged. When he finished his presentation, opposing counsel rose to cross-examine. He leaned slightly towards the witness, dropped his voice to a low baritone, wiggled his eyebrows slightly, and asked the expert, "Sir, do you know anything about the manufacturing process for these batch stamps?"

"No," the witness quickly answered, "and I don't know anything about how they make a fountain pen either."

The jury roared with laughter, and the lawyer sank back in his chair.

Unraveling the other side's story is not only about sizzling cross-examination. It is about figuring out the dots that the other side is trying to connect, and then showing how they do not connect. It is about attacking the credibility and the reliability of the evidence that they present. It is about showing that there are holes in their story, where they wish they had evidence instead. One of the most effective ways of unraveling the opponent's story is by focusing on their own opening statement to the jury. At the beginning of the trial, once the jury has been selected, each lawyer has the opportunity to make an opening statement. It is called a statement, not an argument, because the lawyer is not supposed to "argue" why their side is right or wrong. In the opening statement, the lawyer is only supposed to tell the jury what he believes the evidence will show during the trial. It is a little bit like a jigsaw puzzle, where the jury is going to receive the pieces of evidence at different times and out of logical order, and so the lawyers are allowed to show the jury, before the pieces of evidence come in, what they believe the picture will be when the pieces are put together—just like we look at the box of a jigsaw puzzle before we start trying to make the puzzle. After all of the evidence has been presented, and at the end of the trial, the lawyers are allowed their "closing argument," where they can argue about what the evidence was and why it proves their point.

So, one of the most effective ways to unravel the other side's story is, in closing arguments, to focus on some of the things opposing counsel said in his opening statement. Some of the things opposing counsel <u>promised</u>. He promised that he would prove that certain things happened. He promised that he would show how certain events occurred. He promised that he would prove who was responsible. But he broke his promises. He didn't show you, ladies and gentlemen of the jury, what he told you he was going to show you. You are left to wonder why.

Unraveling the other side's story requires tremendous attention to detail, and mastery of every single piece of evidence in the case, including all of the testimony given by witnesses in depositions, and all of the documents. Some great trial lawyers are bored with or don't have time to handle all of the pretrial activities, and like to step into a case shortly before trial, and after the case has been "worked up" by others. They can often be very effective at this, because they are the masters of the courtroom, they are the lawyers in their firm who know how to connect with the jury, tell a story, and cross-examine a witness. However, the truth is that this approach to trying a case does have its drawbacks, and when the trial lawyer does not truly have mastery of all of the details in the case, that trial lawyer sometimes misses opportunities to unravel the other side's case. There is only so much that can be accomplished, in the heat of trial, by passing notes or whispering in someone's ear. The trial lawyer may have another lawyer sitting right next to him in the courtroom who knows the details, but this sometimes is not enough. It is in the moment of the witness' testimony, when that witness says something that isn't quite consistent with other testimony, or with a document, that the opportunity is created, and perhaps lost, to unravel the other side's case.

Some cases are, in part or in whole, a battle of experts. There is a particular art to trying to unravel the other side's expert, and much of this is very specific to the type of expert you are dealing with, and the facts of your case. In general, find out everything you can about this expert, and particularly, what positions they have taken before and what testimony they have given before. Look hard at how reliable the "science" is behind the conclusions that they give, and pay particular attention to the assumptions that they express. Most expert will give opinions, assuming certain facts to be true. For example, in trying to prove a company's damages because of an interruption in their business activities, the lawyer will present evidence about different aspects of the company's operations and prof- itability; evidence which may be hotly contested by the other side. The lawyer will then present an expert witness, perhaps an accountant or economist, or an expert in that particular industry. The expert will be asked to assume that those facts presented by the lawyer are true, and then ask, if they are true, to express an opinion as to the company's losses. This is perfectly proper, and then will allow the lawyer to argue to the jury that he has proven those facts, and that an expert has told them how much the damages are as a result. In unraveling this story, and attacking this expert, the simplest cross-examination may be to ask the expert, very simply, whether his opinions would be com- pletely different if he assumed different facts. By getting the expert to admit that, if he assumes the facts as you believe them to be, his opinion would be completely different, you make it clear to the jury that they cannot rely upon this expert in order to decide what actually happened. You establish that this expert does not really have personal knowledge of what the facts were. The expert is like a cheap computer—garbage in, garbage out. If there is any part of the other side's story that isn't completely accurate, the expert's opinion can be totally disregarded.

In the end, remember that the other side also has its **themes** and its **theory of the case**. Unravel those, and the jury may be left with no choice but to buy into yours.

Selling Your Story

We have reviewed in some detail the importance of developing, early on, your **themes** and **theory of the case**. We have reviewed how these two aspects of your story are developed throughout the pretrial process, and how you will use your key storytellers, your documentary evidence, and your expert witnesses to reinforce and hammer in every piece of the puzzle. We have talked about how the lawyer, as the grand storyteller, will use all of his storytelling skills, including visualization, to tell a simple and compelling story that is clear, believable, interesting, and understood by the jury. With each of your storytellers, including your lawyer, two critical factors will be **credibility** and **likeability**. These two factors will determine the extent to which your storytellers connect with the jury, whether the jury believes them, and whether the jury cares.

Your **themes** have to be carefully selected, have to be

consistently developed throughout every aspect of the evidence, and have to be framed in a way that common people will connect with. The themes define who the players in the drama are, what their behavior was, and what their motivations were. Your themes are defined so that if the jury buys into them, the trial is headed your way like a rushing train. People are defined by themes: is little Johnny a young student, or a juvenile delinquent; was the security guard large and aggressive or seasoned and professional; was the supervisor demanding and fair, or a bully and a nitpicker. Themes define the parties' actions as well; do mistakes result from being human, or from being reckless. Do several mistakes form a pattern of recklessness? Do random clerical errors become a pattern of miscalculation, or even a pattern of corporate indifference? Finally, themes also define the motivations of parties, and even when those motivations are not necessarily all that relevant, they can have a real impact on a jury's attitude about the case. For example, if you simply breach a contract, it usually doesn't matter why you breached the contract; a breach is a breach, and you owe the other side the damages that they are able to prove resulting from that breach. However, from a practical standpoint, if the jury believes that your motivation for breaching the contract was excessive greed or ill will, they may not only call the close questions against you on the issue of liability, but they may ignore the logic of your expert's testimony on damages, or the excessiveness of the plaintiff's damage demand, and simply give them whatever they ask for.

The key with your **theory of the case** is, in the addition to having one, that you keep it consistent and intact. Your theme should be simple and clear. You cannot waiver from it. You cannot let the other side unravel it.

There's the old joke about the criminal defendant who says "I wasn't there, but even if I was there, I didn't do anything wrong, and if I did something wrong it's because I was told to." Normally, you can't get away with this at trial. You can't have inconsistent theories or alternating theories of what happened. Not if you want to win. Suppose a company is sued for wrongful termination, with the allegation that they fired their employee as a result of racial bias. Suppose further that the employee has no real evidence of any racial motivation behind the decision, or of any racism at the company at all. The company at first takes the position that the employee was simply laid off for economic reasons, because they couldn't afford an employee at that position anymore, and that the position was eliminated. After this, the employee's lawyer shows that there was no economic need, and that the employee was replaced by someone else. Next, the company says that the employee was let go because he wasn't doing a very good job. The plaintiff's lawyer then establishes that the employee worked for the company for many years, and always got positive reviews on the quality of his work. Now, the company tries to establish that the employee, while generally performing good work, had been repeatedly sexually harassing female subordinates, and this was the real reason for his termination. Before any evidence is even considered concerning this supposed sexual harassment, the very fact that the company has repeatedly changed its story on why this person was fired, the very fact that the company's theory of the case has flip-flopped, means two things: (1) the jury is very unlikely to be receptive to this issue of sexual harassment, and far more serious, (2) the jury may now be prepared to completely accept plaintiff's theory that he was fired for racial reasons, even if there isn't a shred of evidence supporting that theory.

Selling your story is about great storytelling, and about setting the story up; it is also about staying on message. Perhaps, above all, it is about maintaining the credibility of your story. The truth is that, at the end of many trials, it is not absolutely clear what happened, or what the details of the events were. The evidence is conflicting, there is no videotape, and there is no certainty. Neither side has been able to prove, definitively, their version of the facts. Often, the winner in this kind of case is the one that wins the "smell test." In a close and tough case, if one side has lost its credibility, even on a minor point, the other side may be believed, even as to things they never did really prove. This can be the price for changing your story, getting caught in a lie, getting caught exaggerating, getting caught trying to hide something, or simply leaving the jury with the impression that you cannot be trusted. It is in these kinds of cases where that great trial lawyer can almost be at a disadvantage against the nervous beginner. The jury sees the evidence as inconclusive, but with one side of the story presented by a slick and capable lawyer, and the other side presented by a bumbling amateur. If the slick lawyer can only get a tie in that contest, maybe the bumbler is right.

Robert M. Dawson

What is marvelous, and maddening, about the trial process is that it is a human process. Human beings put on a re-creation of a mess that was created by other human beings, and then a third set of human beings try to sort out what happened and what they think of it. As Shakespeare said, "Though this be madness, yet there is method in it."

About the Author

Robert M. Dawson is a litigation partner with one of the country's largest and most prestigious law firms emphasizing trial practice. In addition to representing clients in the courtroom, Mr. Dawson devotes substantial time to training young lawyers, and is a faculty member of his firm's renowned Trial Training Program. He has been named repeatedly on lists of "super lawyers."

Robert M. Dawson

Over the course of his career, Mr. Dawson has represented many different types of clients, including large corporations, small companies, public agencies, public officials, wealthy individuals, foreign sovereignty, and charitable institutions. The subjects of his cases have been wide-ranging, including consumer class actions, securities, banking, employment, government, medicine, gaming, organized crime, science and technology, espionage, and entertainment. Mr. Dawson practices and resides in Los Angeles, California.

Requests for additional copies of this book may be directed to rmdawson@fulbright.com